Workbook
and
Audio Activities

Glencoe Spanish 1

¡Buen viaje!

Conrad J. Schmitt
Protase E. Woodford

McGraw Hill Glencoe

New York, New York   Columbus, Ohio   Chicago, Illinois   Peoria, Illinois   Woodland Hills, California

Glencoe

Send all inquiries to:
Glencoe/McGraw-Hill
8787 Orion Place
Columbus, OH 43240-4027

ISBN: 978-0-07-861952-6
MHID: 0-07-861952-1

Printed in the United States of America.

25 24 23 22 21   RHR 15 14 13 12 11

Contents

Workbook

x = 5
mexicana

Capítulo 1

Un amigo o una amiga

Vocabulario   PALABRAS 1

A **Antonio Irizarry**   Here's a picture of Antonio Irizarry. Write a story about him. You may want to use some of the following words.

Colombia	es	serio
Bogotá	no es	rubio
		bajo
		guapo

→ adjective in end clause

Antonio Irizarry es un Colombiano.
El es un guapo muchacho. No es bajo.
El es muy Alto. El no es rubio. El es un
moreno.

B **Una mexicana**   Here's a picture of Guadalupe Cárdenas. She's from Puebla, México. Write as much about her as you can.

La Muchacha Guadalupe
Cárdenas es muy bonita.
No es fea. Ella es una
alumnas seria. Ella no es
tímica. Ella es una mexicana.

_____

_____

_____

¿Es todo? — thats it?

C **Una definición**   Answer the following question to write a definition of the Spanish word colegio.

¿Qué es un colegio?

Un colegio es escuela secundaria

un colegio es lugar para estudiar — (to study)

D **Lo contrario**   Match the opposites. *Place*

1. __d__ alto   **a.** moreno

2. __a__ rubio   **b.** primario

3. __c__ guapo   **c.** feo

4. __e__ serio   **d.** bajo

5. __b__ secundario   **e.** gracioso

E **Robert Walker**   Here's a picture of Robert Walker. Describe him.

Robert Walker es un Muchacho.
El es pelo magro. No es
bajo. El es muy Alto.
El es chido.

F **Carmen de Grávalos**   Here's a picture of Carmen de Grávalos. Describe her.

Carmen de Gravalos es
una mexicana. Ella es
una buena muchacha. NO
es seria alumna. Ella
es perezosa

Vocabulario   PALABRAS 2

G **Yo** Write as much as you can about yourself.

Me nombre es sudhin. sudhin de deletrea muy facile.
Yo soy es Indian. Yo soy flaco y alto. Me pelo
es negro. Me esaila de georgia.

H **Una pregunta** Complete each question with the correct question word(s).

1. *El muchacho* es de Tejas.

¿ _____Quien_____ es de Tejas?

2. *Manolo* es tejano.

¿ _____Quien_____ es tejano?

3. Manolo es *de Houston*.

¿ ___de dunde___ es Manolo?

4. Manolo es *alto y moreno*.

¿ _____Como_____ es Manolo?

5. Manolo es un amigo de *Guadalupe*.

¿ _____Quien_____ es una amiga de Manolo?

I **Juanita Torres** Here's a picture of Juanita Torres. She's from Bogotá, Colombia. Write four questions about her.

1. ___Quien es Muchacha?___
2. ___de dude es Ella?___
3. ___es ella alta y flaca?___
4. ___de que nacionalidad es Juanita Torres?___
   ___Como es Juanita Torres___

J **Don Quijote y Sancho Panza**   Here's a picture of two famous characters in Spanish liter-
ature. Write as much as you can about each of them.

1. Don Quijote ___Don Quijote es un libero famoso.___
___El autor de Don Quijote es Cervantes. El is___
___alto y flaco. No es gordo._____
_____
_____

2. Sancho Panza _____
_____
_____
_____
_____
_____

Estructura

Artículos—el, la, un, una

A   **Oye, ¿quién es?**   Complete the cartoon with **el** or **la**.

B   **Un alumno y una alumna**   Complete the sentences with **un** or **una**.

1. Alan es ___un___ alumno en ___una___ escuela secundaria en Estados Unidos.

2. Alejandra es ___una___ alumna en ___un___ colegio en Olivos, ___un___ suburbio de Buenos Aires.

3. Alejandra es ___una___ persona muy sincera.

4. Y Alan es ___un___ muchacho muy honesto.

Adjetivos en el singular

C **¿Quién es?** Describe the boy.

_____

_____

_____

_____

D **¿Quién es?** Describe the girl.

_____

_____

_____

_____

Presente del verbo **ser** en el singular

E **Yo** Answer the following questions about yourself.

1. ¿Quién eres?

Yo soy Sudhin, soy muchacho.

2. ¿De dónde eres?

_____

3. ¿De qué nacionalidad eres?

Me naciandidad es Indian.

4. ¿Dónde eres alumno(a)?

_____

5. ¿Cómo eres? ¿Qué tipo de persona eres?

_____

6. ¿De quién eres amigo(a)?

_____

F   **Catalina**   This is Catalina. Tell her what you think about her.

Catalina, tú _____

_____

_____

G   **Una tarjeta**   Read this postcard from Claudia de los Ríos.

¡Hola!
Yo soy Claudia de los Ríos.
Soy de La Paz, Bolivia. Soy
boliviana. Soy alumna
en una escuela privada
para muchachas. Soy
una alumna bastante
buena. Soy una persona
sincera, honesta y seria.
Sí, soy seria pero de
ninguna manera soy
aburrida. Soy bastante
graciosa,
    Con cariño,
    Claudia

H   **Claudia**   Write some things Claudia says about herself in her postcard.

_____

_____

_____

I   **Otra tarjeta**   Now write a postcard to Claudia. Tell her all about yourself.

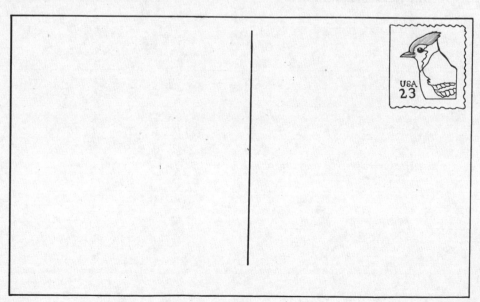

J **¿Quién eres?** A young man has just walked up to you on the street. He recognizes you, but you are not sure who he is. Complete the conversation you are having with this person.

MUCHACHO: Hola, ¿qué tal?

TÚ: Muy bien, gracias. ¿Y tú?

MUCHACHO: Muy bien, gracias. Tú _____ _____ *(your name).*
  1

TÚ: Sí, _____ _____ *(your name).*
  2

MUCHACHO: Tú _____ el/la amigo(a) de Gloria Sánchez, ¿no?
  3

TÚ: Sí, yo _____ un(a) amigo(a) de Gloria Sánchez. Pero, perdón.
  4

¿Quién _____ tú?
  5

MUCHACHO: Yo _____ Tomás. Tomás Smith.
  6

TÚ: Ay, sí. Tú _____ de Miami, ¿no?
  7

MUCHACHO: Sí, yo _____ de Miami. Tú _____ de Ponce, ¿no?
  8   9

TÚ: Si, yo _____ de Ponce y yo _____ amigo(a)
  10   11

de Gloria también. Ella _____ muy simpática, ¿no?
  12

MUCHACHO: Sí, _____ una amiga muy sincera y _____
  13   14

muy graciosa también.

Un poco màs

A **Más información** Every chapter in your workbook will include readings. These readings will have some unfamiliar words in them. However, you should be able to understand them easily, since many of them are cognates—words that look alike and have similar meanings in English and Spanish. In addition, you can guess the meanings of other words because of the context of the sentence. See whether you can understand the following reading.

> Simón Bolívar es un héroe famoso de Latinoamérica. Es de una familia noble y rica. No es de la ciudad. Simón Bolívar es de una región rural. Es del campo.
>
> En la época de Simón Bolívar, Venezuela es una colonia de España. No es un país independiente. La mayoría de Latinoamérica es una colonia española. Las ideas de Simón Bolívar son muy liberales. Para él, Venezuela no debe[1] ser una colonia. Venezuela debe ser un país independiente.
>
> [1]debe *should*

B **En inglés** Give the English word related to each of the following Spanish words. As you already know, these related words are called "cognates."

1. héroe _____

2. famoso _____

3. noble _____

4. región rural _____

5. colonia _____

6. independiente _____

Mi autobiografía

Begin to write your autobiography in Spanish. You will have fun adding to it as you continue
with your study of Spanish. To begin, tell who you are and where you are from. Indicate your
nationality and tell where you are a student. Also, give a brief description of yourself. What
do you look like? How would you describe your personality?

Mi autobiografía

Capítulo 2
Alumnos y cursos

Vocabulario   PALABRAS 1

A **La clase** Answer the following questions based on the illustration.

1. ¿Hay muchos alumnos en la clase?

   _____

2. ¿Es una clase grande o pequeña?

   _____

3. ¿Es una clase interesante o aburrida?

   _____

4. ¿Quién es el profesor?

   _____

Nombre _____ Fecha _____

B **La clase** Write a short paragraph describing the class in the illustration on page 11.

_____

_____

_____

_____

_____

_____

C **Una pregunta** Choose the correct question word.

1. Ella es Maricarmen.

Perdón, ¿ _____ es ella?

a. cómo

b. de dónde

c. quién

2. Maricarmen es chilena.

Perdón, ¿ _____ es ella?

a. cómo

b. quién

c. qué

3. Ella es de Santiago.

Perdón, ¿ _____ es ella?

a. quién

b. cómo

c. de dónde

4. Ella es alumna.

Perdón, ¿ _____ es ella?

a. cómo

b. qué

c. quién

5. Ella es alumna en el Colegio San José.

Perdón, ¿ _____ es alumna?

a. cómo

b. dónde

c. qué

6. Maricarmen y Teresa son buenas amigas.

Perdón, ¿ _____ son amigas?

a. qué

b. quiénes

c. cómo

Nombre _____ Fecha _____

Vocabulario   PALABRAS 2

D **¿Qué son?** Complete each sentence with an appropriate word.

1. La biología, la química y la física son _____.

2. El inglés, el español, el chino y el ruso son _____.

3. El latín es una _____ antigua.

4. El francés y el español son _____ modernas.

5. La _____, la geografía y la sociología son ciencias sociales.

6. La zoología y la botánica son partes de la _____.

7. El fútbol, el voleibol y el básquetbol son partes de la _____.

8. El álgebra, la geometría y el cálculo son partes de las _____.

E **Alumnos, profesores y cursos** Indicate whether each statement is true or false. Write **sí** or **no.**

1. _____ Los alumnos serios son estudiosos.

2. _____ Los alumnos buenos no son estudiosos.

3. _____ Los profesores interesantes son aburridos.

4. _____ Los profesores aburridos son buenos.

5. _____ Los profesores simpáticos son populares con los alumnos.

6. _____ Los cursos interesantes son populares con los alumnos.

F **Los cursos** Write the names of all the courses you are taking this year.

_____

_____

G **¿Cómo son los cursos?** Rate your courses using the following words.

difícil   **fácil**   **aburrido**   **interesante**

_____

_____

_____

Estructura

Sustantivos, artículos y adjetivos en el plural

A **Julia y Alejandra** Look at the illustration of Julia and Alejandra. They are from Bogotá, Colombia. Write four sentences about them.

1. _____

2. _____

3. _____

4. _____

B **Armando y Héctor** Armando and Héctor are from Bogotá, too. Write four sentences about them.

1. _____

2. _____

3. _____

4. _____

Presente de **ser** en el plural

C **El plural, por favor.** Rewrite each sentence in the plural.

1. El muchacho es inteligente y serio.

_____

2. La muchacha es inteligente y graciosa.

_____

3. El muchacho es el amigo de Teresa.

_____

4. El profesor inteligente es interesante.

_____

5. El curso es interesante pero es difícil.

_____

D **Una carta** Complete the following letter in which you talk about yourself and your friend Fernando.

> *Fernando y yo _____ amigos.*
> 1
> *Nosotros _____ americanos.*
> 2
> *_____ alumnos en una escuela*
> 3
> *secundaria. _____ alumnos en*
> 4
> *la Escuela Martin Luther King.*

E **El hermano de Ana Sofía** Complete the conversation with the correct form of **ser.**

Hola, Isabel. ¿Quién _____ el muchacho?

_____ Justo. Él _____ el hermano de Ana Sofía.

Ah, ¿él y Ana Sofía _____ hermanos?

Sí, y _____ alumnos en la Escuela Internacional.

Tú también _____ alumna en la Escuela Internacional, ¿no?

Sí, nosotros tres _____ alumnos en la misma escuela.

¿ _____ Uds. amigos?

Sí, _____ muy buenos amigos.

La hora

F   **¿Qué hora es?** Write a sentence telling the time on each clock.

1. _____

2. _____

3. _____

4. _____

5. _____

6. _____

7. _____

8. _____

WORKBOOK

Un poco màs

A **Civilizaciones indígenas** Read the following. Try to guess the words you do not know.

En muchas partes de Latinoamérica hay influencias importantes de los indios de las poblaciones indígenas. Antes de la llegada[1] de Cristóbal Colón a las Américas, los habitantes de la América del Norte, de la América Central y de la América del Sur son los indios.

Hoy hay descendientes de los famosos aztecas y mayas en México, Guatemala y otras partes de la América Central.

En países[2] como Ecuador, Perú y Bolivia hay muchos descendientes de los incas. Y más al sur en Chile hay descendientes de los araucanos. Pero hay muy pocos. No quedan[3] muchos descendientes de los araucanos.

[1] llegada *arrival*
[2] países *countries*
[3] quedan *remain*

B **Grupos indígenas** Make a list of Indian or indigenous groups mentioned in the preceding story.

_____

_____

_____

C **Países** Make a list of the countries mentioned in the story.

_____

_____

_____

D **¿Descendientes de quiénes?** Indicate the indigenous group that lives in each country.

_____

_____

_____

_____

Mi autobiografía

Continue with your autobiography. Write a list of the courses you are taking now. Tell who the teacher of each class is. Describe each course. Tell which ones are interesting, boring, easy, or difficult. Then tell something about your school friends. What are they like?

Mi autobiografía

Capítulo 3

Las compras para la escuela

Vocabulario   PALABRAS 1

A **Materiales escolares** Write in Spanish a list of things you'll need in order to do each of the following activities.

1. You are going to write a composition for your English class.

_____

_____

2. You are going to do your algebra homework.

_____

_____

3. You are going to take some notes in your history class.

_____

_____

B **Tomás necesita mucho.** Make up a sentence using each of the following words.

1. necesita _____

2. busca _____

3. mira _____

4. habla _____

5. compra _____

6. paga _____

C **En la papelería** Answer the following questions according to the illustration.

1. ¿Dónde está Juan Carlos?

_____

2. ¿Qué mira en la papelería?

_____

3. ¿Qué compra?

_____

4. ¿Con quién habla?

_____

5. ¿Cuánto es la carpeta?

_____

6. ¿Dónde paga Juan Carlos?

_____

7. ¿En qué lleva Juan Carlos los materiales escolares?

_____

Vocabulario   PALABRAS 2

D   **La ropa** Answer the questions according to the illustrations.

1. ¿Qué lleva el muchacho?

_____

_____

2. ¿Qué lleva la muchacha?

_____

_____

E   **A casa de una amiga** Write what Alejandra is putting in her backpack.

       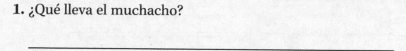   

1. _____   2. _____   3. _____   4. _____

5. _____   6. _____   7. _____   8. _____

F **Conversaciones** Complete the following short conversations.

1. En la tienda de ropa

—Sí, señor. ¿Qué _____ usted?

—Una camisa, por _____.

—¿De qué _____?

—Blanca, por favor.

—Sí, señor. No hay problema. ¿Qué _____ usa usted?

—Treinta y ocho.

2. En la tienda de zapatos

—Sí, señorita. ¿Qué _____ usted?

—Un _____ de tenis, por favor.

—Sí, señorita. ¿De qué _____?

—Blanco y azul, por favor.

—¿Y qué _____ usa usted?

—Treinta y seis.

3. En la caja

—¿Cuánto _____ la camisa?

—Quinientos pesos.

—¡Quinientos pesos! _____ mucho, ¿no?

—Sí, es bastante cara.

G **Colores favoritos** Give your favorite color or colors for the following items of clothing.

1. los tenis _____

2. una camisa _____

3. una camiseta _____

4. los zapatos _____

5. una gorra _____

Estructura

Presente de los verbos en -ar en el singular

A **Preguntas personales** Answer each of the following questions.

1. ¿Qué materiales escolares necesitas para la apertura de clases?

   _____

2. ¿Qué compras en la papelería?

   _____

3. ¿Qué llevas a la escuela?

   _____

4. ¿Dónde compras la ropa?

   _____

5. ¿Con quién hablas en la tienda de ropa?

   _____

6. Si compras una camiseta, ¿qué talla usas?

   _____

7. Si compras un par de zapatos, ¿qué número usas?

   _____

8. En la tienda, ¿dónde pagas?

   _____

9. ¿Cuesta mucho o poco la ropa?

   _____

10. ¿Es cara o barata la ropa?

   _____

B **Conversaciones** Complete the following conversations with the verbs in parentheses.

1. —¿Qué _____ usted, señorita? (desear)

   —Yo _____ un par de zapatos. (necesitar)

   —¿Qué número _____ usted? (usar)

   —Treinta y ocho.

   La señora _____ un par de zapatos. Ella _____

   los zapatos y _____ en la caja. (mirar, comprar, pagar)

2. —Hola, Paco. ¿Qué _____ hoy? (necesitar)

   —Pues, _____ una calculadora para la clase de álgebra. (necesitar)

   —¿Qué tal la clase de álgebra?

   —Muy bien. Pero es un poco difícil.

   Paco _____ varias calculadoras y _____ una.
   (mirar, seleccionar)

   —¿Cuánto _____ la calculadora? (ser)

   La calculadora _____ un poco cara pero Paco _____

   la calculadora y _____ en la caja. (ser, comprar, pagar)

Tú o usted

C **Preguntas** Make up three questions you want to ask one of your teachers.

1. _____

2. _____

3. _____

Now write the same questions, but address them to a good friend.

4. _____

5. _____

6. _____

Un poco màs

A **¿Qué lleva?** Look at the clothing advertisement that appeared recently in the newspaper *El Nuevo Día* in San Juan, Puerto Rico.

VENTA 69.99
Reg. $92. Conjunto de pantalón Perceptions® con blusa en diseños de rayas a colores.

Answer the questions according to the advertisement.

1. ¿Qué lleva la muchacha?

_____

2. ¿Cuál es el precio regular del pantalón con la blusa?

_____

3. ¿Cuál es el precio especial?

_____

Nombre _____ Fecha _____

La ropa Look at the following advertisements for some men's clothing that appeared recently in the newspaper *El Nuevo Día* in San Juan, Puerto Rico.

$13

CAMISAS PARA CABALLEROS.
Estilo de mangas cortas con banda.
Tallas S-XL. Regular 17.99.

$13

PANTALONES CORTOS
Tallas 30- 42. Regular 15.99.

$16

MAHONES
COMFORT
ACTION
PARA ÉL
Regular
19.99-21.99.
Tallas
grandes
44-50,
Regular
21.99,
VENTA $18

$7

NOVEDOSAS
CAMISETAS
PARA ÉL
Tallas
S-XL.
Reg. 9.99.
Otros estilos,
Reg. 6.99,
VENTA $6

Choose the correct completion for each statement according to the information in the ads.

1. El precio regular de los pantalones cortos es _____.

   a. $13   **b.** $15.99   **c.** $16

2. En Puerto Rico los mahones son _____.

   a. pantalones cortos   **b.** blue jeans   **c.** camisetas

3. Hay también tallas grandes para _____.

   a. las camisas   **b.** los pantalones cortos   **c.** los mahones

4. Hay varios estilos de _____.

   a. camisas   **b.** camisetas   **c.** mahones

C **Los materiales escolares** Look at the following advertisement for stationery items.

Find the Spanish equivalent for the following terms.

1. school agenda _____

2. spiral notebook _____

D Answer the following questions according to the information in the ads in Activity C.

1. ¿Cuál es el nombre de la papelería?

_____

2. ¿Cuántos departamentos hay en la carpeta clasificadora?

_____

Mi autobiografía

Continue with your autobiography. Describe what for you is a typical outfit of clothing. Tell what you wear to school. Tell some things you do to get ready for back to school—**la apertura de clases.**

Mi autobiografía

Capítulo 4
En la escuela

Vocabulario   PALABRAS 1

A **La escuela** Complete each statement with an appropriate word.

1. Los alumnos _____ a la escuela a eso de las ocho menos cuarto de la mañana.

2. Algunos toman el _____ escolar y otros van en

_____ o a _____.

3. Los alumnos entran en la _____.

4. Ahora los _____ están en la sala de clase.

5. En la escuela los alumnos _____ y los profesores

_____.

B **A la escuela** Answer each of the following questions.

1. ¿A qué hora llegan los alumnos a la escuela?

_____

2. ¿Cómo van a la escuela?

_____

3. ¿Dónde estudian los alumnos?

_____

4. ¿Quién enseña?

_____

Vocabulario   PALABRAS 2

C **¿Qué es?** Identify each item.

 1. _____

 2. _____

 3. _____

 4. _____

 5. _____

D **Actividades escolares** Complete each statement with an appropriate word.

1. Los alumnos _____ en la sala de clase.

2. El profesor _____ y los alumnos _____.

3. Los alumnos prestan _____ cuando el _____ habla.

4. A veces los alumnos _____ apuntes.

5. A veces el profesor _____ un examen. Los alumnos

_____ el examen.

6. Los alumnos que _____ mucho sacan una nota

_____ y los alumnos que no estudian mucho sacan una nota

_____.

E **Una fiesta** Write several sentences describing the illustration.

_____

_____

_____

_____

_____

F **Preguntas** Complete each question with the correct question word.

1. Los alumnos estudian.

¿ _____ estudian?

2. Los alumnos van a la escuela.

¿ _____ van los alumnos?

3. Ahora los alumnos están en la sala de clase.

¿ _____ están los alumnos ahora?

4. El profesor enseña a los alumnos.

¿ _____ enseña a los alumnos?

5. El profesor da un examen.

¿ _____ da el profesor?

6. El examen es difícil.

¿ _____ es el examen?

Estructura

Presente de los verbos en **-ar** en el plural

A **Vamos a la escuela.** Complete each sentence with the correct form of the verb(s) in parentheses.

1. Los alumnos _____ a la escuela. (llegar)

2. Algunos _____ el bus escolar. (tomar)

3. Ellos _____ en la escuela. (entrar)

4. En la sala de clase los alumnos _____ al profesor y

   _____ apuntes. (escuchar, tomar)

5. Ellos _____ atención cuando el profesor _____.
   (prestar, hablar)

B **Nosotros también** Rewrite the sentences from Activity A in paragraph form using **nosotros.**

Nosotros _____

_____

_____

C **Un día en la escuela** Make up sentences using a word from each category.

Yo	estudiar	al profesor
Los alumnos	tomar	en la clase
Ustedes	escuchar	a la escuela
Nosotros	mirar	mucho
Usted	llegar	la pizarra
Ella	entrar	apuntes

1. _____

2. _____

3. _____

4. _____

5. _____

6. _____

WORKBOOK
Copyright © by The McGraw-Hill Companies, Inc.

Presente de los verbos **ir, dar, estar**

D **Tres veces, por favor.** Answer each question three times according to the illustrations.

1. ¿Adónde vas?

a. _____

b. _____

c. _____

Cómo vas?

_____

b. _____

c. _____

3. ¿Dónde estás ahora?

a. _____

b. _____

c. _____

E   **¿Dónde estoy?** Write where you are when you do each of the following activities.

Tomas un examen.
Estoy en la escuela cuando tomo un examen.

1. Tomas una merienda.

_____

_____

2. Compras un bolígrafo.

_____

_____

3. Estudias español.

_____

_____

4. Pagas.

_____

_____

5. Compras un blue jean.

_____

_____

F   **¿Qué profesor?** Complete each sentence with the correct form of the verb in parentheses.

1. El profesor de biología _____ muchos exámenes. (dar)

2. El profesor de inglés y el profesor de historia no _____ muchos exámenes. (dar)

3. Desde las tres hasta las cuatro el profesor de biología siempre _____ en el laboratorio. (estar)

4. Él _____ al laboratorio para preparar las lecciones. (ir)

5. A veces yo _____ al laboratorio. (ir)

6. Cuando yo _____ en el laboratorio, trabajo con un microscopio. (estar)

G **¿Y ustedes?** Complete each conversation with the correct form of the verb in parentheses.

1. dar

—¿Tú _____ una fiesta?

—¿Quién? ¿Yo? No, yo no _____ una fiesta. ¿De qué fiesta hablas?

2. ir

—¿Tú _____ a la fiesta de Marta?

—Sí, _____. ¿Tú _____ también?

—¡Claro! Yo _____ con Sandra.

—¿Cómo _____ ustedes?

—Nosotros _____ en carro.

3. estar

—Roberto, ¿cómo _____?

—_____ bien.

—¿Tú _____ bien? ¿Seguro?

—Pues, así, así. _____ nervioso.

—¿Por qué?

—Porque mañana es el examen final de español.

Nombre _____   Fecha _____

Las contracciones **al** y **del**

H **Frases originales** Make up sentences using a word from each category.

| Miro / Miramos | el / la / al / a la | empleado / video / carpeta / profesora |

1. _____

2. _____

3. _____

4. _____

| Vamos | al / a la / a los / a las | caja / fiesta / laboratorios / papelería / clases / colegio / escuela / tiendas / café |

5. _____

6. _____

7. _____

8. _____

9. _____

10. _____

11. _____

12. _____

Un poco màs

A **Las notas** Look at Elena's report card. Give the following information according to her report card.

INSTITUTO NACIONAL DE BACHILLERATO
"SANTA TERESA DE JESÚS"
Fomento, núm 9 • MADRID • 13

EXPLICACIÓN DE SIGLAS

C: Conocimientos.

SB	Sobresaliente
NT	Notable
B	Bien.
SF	Suficiente.
IS	Insuficiente.
MD	Muy deficiente.

Ac: Actitud.

A	Muy buena
B	Buena
C	Normal
D	Pasiva
E	Negativa

BOLETÍN DE NOTAS

DE LA ALUMNA
Elena Ruíz de las Rivas
Lope de Vega, 90
GB - 0976

Curso C. O. U.
Grupo **1**

CURSO ACADÉMICO

_____ 19 _____

Escobar de Cruz

DE VISITAS DE PADRES
Horas:

ALUMNA Elena Ruíz de las Rivas Número **26** Curso C. O. U.

SESIONES DE EVALUACIÓN

MATERIAS

	1ª			2ª		
	C	Ac	AG	C	Ac	AG
Seminario de Lengua Española	NT	B	S	NT	B	S
Filosofía	SB	A	S	SB	A	S
Lengua Extranjera Inglés	B	B	S	SF	B	S
Literatura	B	C	RC	B	C	RC
H.ª del Mundo Contemporáneo	NT	B	S	NT	B	S
Latín						
Griego				B	A	S
H. ª del Arte	SF	C	RC	SF	B	RC
Matemáticas	B	B	S			
Física				SB	A	S
Química	NT	A	S	NT	B	S
Biología	B	C	RA	IS	D	RR
Geología	SF	D				
Dibujo Técnico						

1. en qué escuela estudia _____

2. qué cursos toma _____

_____

3. qué nota saca en español _____

4. qué nota saca en matemáticas _____

B **Actitud** Look at Elena's report card again. Write the terms used to describe a student's attitude.

1. _____   4. _____

2. _____   5. _____

3. _____

WORKBOOK

C **Conocimiento** Look at the report card again. Write the terms used to describe a student's achievement.

1. _____   4. _____

2. _____   5. _____

3. _____   6. _____

D **Estudio de palabras** When you learn one word, it is often easy to recognize and guess the meaning of another word that is related to it. Observe the following and see if you can understand the new words used in each sentence.

1. la escuela / escolar
   Los alumnos llevan los materiales escolares a la escuela.
2. enseñar / la enseñanza
   Los profesores enseñan. La enseñanza es la profesión de los profesores.
3. estudiar / el estudio
   Los alumnos estudian la biología. La biología es el estudio de las plantas y los animales.
4. apuntar / los apuntes
   Los alumnos toman apuntes cuando el profesor habla. El profesor apunta algo importante en una hoja de papel.
5. cantar / el (la) cantante / la canción
   El cantante canta una canción bonita.
6. bailar / el (la) bailador(a) / el baile
   El baile que bailan los bailadores es la rumba cubana.

E Look at the following advertisement that appeared recently in the newspaper *El Nuevo Día* in San Juan, Puerto Rico. Then answer the following questions in English.

1. What do the young people have in their hands?

_____

2. What is the advertisement looking for?

_____

Mi autobiografía

Continue with your autobiography. Write about a typical school day. Tell some things you do in school each day. Describe your school and some of your classes and clubs.

Mi autobiografía

WORKBOOK

CHECK-UP 1

A   Identify each item.

1. _____

2. _____

3. _____

4. _____

5. _____

6. _____

7. _____

8. _____

B Answer the following questions.

1. ¿Cuántos cursos tomas?

_____

2. ¿Estudias el español?

_____

3. ¿Qué cursos son fáciles y qué cursos son difíciles?

_____

4. ¿Cómo es el profesor o la profesora de español?

_____

5. ¿Qué compran los alumnos en la papelería?

_____

6. ¿En qué llevan ustedes los materiales escolares a la escuela?

_____

7. ¿Llevas una camiseta y un par de tenis a la escuela?

_____

8. ¿Quiénes prestan atención cuando el profesor habla en clase?

_____

C Complete each sentence with the correct form of the verb(s) in parentheses.

1. ¡Hola! Yo _____ *(your name).* (ser)

2. Nosotros _____ alumnos. (ser)

3. Nosotros _____ en la Escuela Franklin. (estudiar)

4. ¿Dónde _____ ustedes? (estudiar)

5. Yo _____ cinco cursos. ¿Cuántos cursos _____ tú?
(tomar, tomar)

6. Algunos cursos _____ fáciles y otros _____ difíciles.
(ser, ser)

7. ¿En qué clase _____ tú ahora? (estar)

8. Yo _____ en la clase de español pero ahora _____ a
la clase de álgebra.   (estar, ir)

9. El viernes el Club de español _____ una fiesta y todos nosotros

_____. (dar, ir)

D Combine the following words to make a sentence as in the model.

curso / interesante / difícil
El curso es interesante y difícil.

1. clase / aburrido / difícil

_____

2. lenguas / fácil

_____

3. muchacha / guapo / simpático

_____

4. muchachos / guapo / popular

_____

WORKBOOK
Copyright © by The McGraw-Hill Companies, Inc.

¡**Buen viaje! Level 1 Check-Up 1**   **43**

E Complete each sentence with the appropriate word(s).

1. Miramos _____ video.

2. Miramos _____ profesor y escuchamos _____ profesor cuando él habla en clase.

3. Vamos _____ fiesta _____ Club de español.

4. Hablamos _____ clase de biología.

F Give the following information.

1. un suburbio de Lima _____

2. la capital de Venezuela _____

3. cuando es la apertura de clases en Madrid _____

Capítulo 5
En el café

Vocabulario

PALABRAS 1

 ¿Qué es? Identify each item and indicate whether it is **para comer** or **para beber**.

1

2

3

4

5

6

7

Para comer

_____

_____

_____

_____

Para beber

_____

_____

_____

_____

B   **En el café** Complete the following conversation with the appropriate words.

—¿Qué _____ ustedes?

1

—Para _____, un café solo, por favor.

2

—Y para mí, _____, por favor.

3

—Deseo pagar _____, por favor.

4

—Sí, señor. Enseguida.

—¿Está incluido _____?

5

—Sí, señor.

C   **¿Hay una mesa?** Complete the following paragraph with the appropriate words.

Cuando el/la cliente llega a un café _____ una mesa libre. Cuando

1

_____ una mesa libre, toma la mesa. El mesero llega a la mesa. El/La

2

cliente _____ el menú y el mesero _____ la orden.

3   4

Vocabulario   PALABRAS 2

D **¿Qué es?** Identify each item.

1. _____

2. _____

3. _____

4. _____

5. _____

6. _____

7. _____

Nombre _____ Fecha _____

E 🔲 **Comidas** Answer each question.

1. ¿Cuáles son las tres comidas del día?

_____

2. ¿En qué comida tomamos un café o chocolate caliente y un pan dulce o cereal?

_____

3. En Estados Unidos, ¿cuál es la comida principal?

_____

4. ¿En qué comida come la gente un sándwich o una ensalada?

_____

F 🔲 **En el mercado** Complete the following conversation.

—¿ _____ están las manzanas hoy?
          1

—_____ a veinte pesos _____ kilo.
      2   3

—Un kilo, por favor.

—¿ _____, señora?
          4

—No, _____ más, gracias.
          5

—Luego, un kilo de _____. Son veinte pesos.
                         6

G 🔲 **¿Qué es?** Identify each item.

1. _____

2. _____

3. _____

Estructura

Presente de los verbos en -er e -ir

A **Frases** Match the verb in the left-hand column with the appropriate word(s) in the right-hand column.

1. _____ leer   **a.** el menú

2. _____ escribir   **b.** un bocadillo

3. _____ beber   **c.** en Madrid

4. _____ comer   **d.** el inglés en la escuela

5. _____ vivir   **e.** la orden

6. _____ aprender   **f.** una limonada

B **Alejandra** Write sentences about Alejandra, using the phrases from Activity A.

1. _____

2. _____

3. _____

4. _____

5. _____

6. _____

C **Los dos amigos** Rewrite the sentences from Activity B, changing **Alejandra** to **Los dos amigos.**

1. _____

2. _____

3. _____

4. _____

5. _____

6. _____

D **Personalmente** Answer the following questions.

1. ¿Dónde vives?

   _____

   _____

2. ¿Viven ustedes en un apartamento?

   _____

   _____

3. ¿Comen ustedes en la cafetería de la escuela?

   _____

   _____

4. ¿Qué comes en (para) el almuerzo?

   _____

   _____

5. ¿Leen ustedes mucho?

   _____

   _____

6. ¿En qué clase lees tú mucho?

   _____

   _____

7. ¿Escribes muchas composiciones?

   _____

   _____

8. ¿Para qué clase escriben ustedes muchas composiciones?

   _____

   _____

E **En la escuela** Complete each mini-conversation with the correct form of the verb in parentheses.

1. (comprender)

—Oye, Sandra, ¿ _____ tú la lección?

—Sí, _____ la lección.

2. (aprender)

—Sandra, ¿ _____ mucho en la escuela?

—Sí, sí. _____ mucho.

3. (recibir)

—Sandra, ¿ _____ (tú) notas muy altas?

—Pues, a veces _____ notas altas pero no siempre.

4. (escribir)

—Sandra y Tomás, ¿ _____ ustedes muchas composiciones para la clase de inglés?

—Sí, _____ muchas.

5. (comprender)

—Sandra y Tomás, ¿ _____ ustedes las instrucciones en el laboratorio de física?

—Sí, _____ las instrucciones.

F **En el café** Answer according to the illustration.

1. ¿Hay muchos o pocos clientes en el café?

_____

2. ¿Hay muchas o pocas mesas libres?

_____

3. ¿Hay una mesa libre para los clientes que llegan ahora?

_____

4. ¿Hay un menú en la mesa?

_____

5. ¿Hay pizzas en el menú?

_____

Un poco màs

A **Un anuncio** Read the following advertisement for a fast-food restaurant that appeared in the Puerto Rican newspaper *El Nuevo Día.*

B **Preguntas** Answer the questions according to the information in the ad in Activity A.

1. ¿Cuánto cuesta el desayuno? _____

2. Y el almuerzo, ¿cuánto cuesta? _____

3. ¿Para qué días de la semana es válida la oferta especial? _____

4. ¿Qué no está incluido en la oferta? _____

C **A escoger** Look at the ad in Activity A again. Label each of the following items by writing the appropriate letter alongside each item.

1. _____ una ensalada   **4.** _____ panqueques

2. _____ dos huevos fritos   **5.** _____ una hamburguesa

3. _____ un sándwich club   **6.** _____ papas fritas

D **El menú** Look at the menu from a fast-food restaurant in Madrid.

E **Adivinen.** There are many words in the menu in this ad that you already know. There are some, however, that you do not know. Find the Spanish equivalent for the following.

1. cream cheese _____

2. mayonnaise _____

3. salmon _____

4. tomato slices _____

5. asparagus _____

6. grilled chicken _____

7. barbecue sauce _____

8. mineral water _____

9. juices _____

WORKBOOK

Nombre _____ Fecha _____

F **Comestibles** Read the ads for food that appeared in some Spanish and Mexican newspapers.

G **Los precios** Look at the ads in Activity F again and give the price of the following items.

1. tres latas de atún en aceite vegetal _____

2. cuatro latas de salsa de tomate _____

3. una bolsa de cinco libras de papas _____

4. una botella de aceite de oliva _____

Mi autobiografía

Continue with your autobiography. Tell where you live. Describe some things you do after school. Do you go to a café with some friends? Tell what you eat and drink. Tell some things about your daily routine. When do you eat each meal and what do you usually eat?

Mi autobiografía

Capítulo 6
La familia y su casa

Vocabulario   PALABRAS 1

A **El árbol genealógico** Write the relationship of each person to Alejandra.

B **Una familia** Complete each sentence with the appropriate word(s).

1. Una familia grande tiene muchas _____ y una familia pequeña tiene

   pocas _____.

2. Una persona que tiene catorce años es _____ y una persona que tiene

   noventa años es _____.

3. Muchas familias tienen un _____ o un gato.

4. El _____ y el _____ son animales domésticos.

C   **El cumpleaños** Complete with the appropriate words.

Hoy es el _____ de Diana. Ella _____ catorce

             1   2

años. Sus padres dan una _____ en su honor para celebrar su

                                  3

_____. Los padres _____ a los amigos y a los

        4   5

parientes de Diana a la fiesta. Diana recibe muchos _____.

                                                               6

Vocabulario   PALABRAS 2

D   **Los cuartos** Label the rooms of the house.

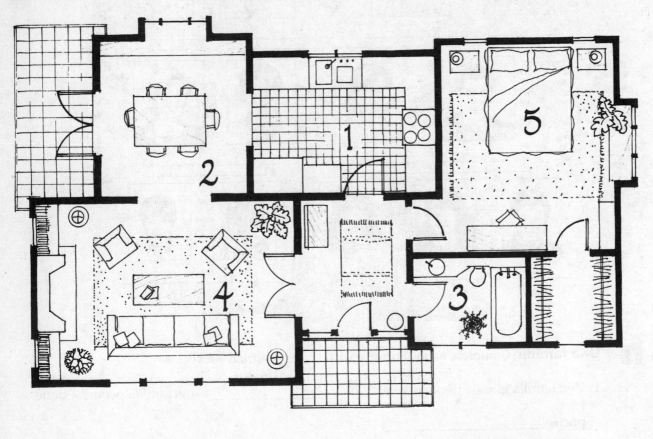

1. _____   4. _____

2. _____   5. _____

3. _____

E **La casa** Identify each item.

1. _____   2. _____

3. _____   4. _____

5. _____   6. _____

F **Actividades familiares** Complete each sentence with the appropriate word.

1. La familia _____ en el comedor.

2. La familia prepara la comida en la _____.

3. La familia mira (ve) la televisión en la _____.

4. José estudia o escucha la radio en su _____.

5. La familia lee el _____ en la sala.

Nombre _____ Fecha _____

Personalmente Give your own answers.

1. Cuando tú ves la televisión, ¿qué tipo de emisiones ves?

_____

2. Cuando lees, ¿qué lees?

_____

En casa Write as much about the illustration as you can.

_____

_____

_____

_____

_____

_____

_____

Estructura

Presente de **tener**

A   **Más preguntas personales** Give your own answers.

1. ¿Cuántos hermanos tienes?

_____

2. ¿Tienes tíos?

_____

3. ¿Tienes primos? Si tienes primos, ¿cuántos tienes?

_____

4. ¿Tienes abuelos?

_____

5. ¿Cuántos años tienes?

_____

6. ¿Tienes una mascota (un animal doméstico)?

_____

7. Si tienes una mascota, ¿qué tienes?

_____

B   **La edad** Give the age of each member of your immediate family.

_____

_____

_____

_____

_____

C **¿Qué tiene?** Tell what each person has.

1. Ella / perro

_____

2. Ellos / coche grande

_____

3. Yo / bicicleta

_____

4. Nosotros / casa privada

_____

5. Ustedes / apartamento elegante

_____

6. Tú / mucho dinero

_____

Tener que; Ir a

D **Es necesario.** Answer each question.

1. ¿Tienes que escribir composiciones para la clase de inglés?

_____

2. ¿Tienen ustedes que hablar español en la clase de español?

_____

3. ¿A qué hora tienen que llegar los alumnos a la escuela?

_____

4. ¿Qué tiene que preparar un miembro de la familia en la cocina?

_____

5. ¿Qué tienes que comprar para el cumpleaños de un(a) pariente?

_____

E **Mañana** Tell what each person is going to do tomorrow. Use **ir a.**

1. Yo doy una fiesta en honor de Adela.

_____

2. Paco cumple quince años.

_____

3. Tú escribes una composición para la clase de español.

_____

4. Los padres invitan a los abuelos a comer.

_____

5. Nosotros compramos un regalo para la abuela.

_____

Adjetivos posesivos

F **Preguntas personales** Give your own answers.

1. ¿Dónde viven tus abuelos?

_____

2. ¿Cuántos hijos tiene tu abuela materna?

_____

3. ¿Dónde trabaja tu madre o tu padre?

_____

4. ¿Tienes hermanos? ¿A qué escuela van tus hermanos? Si no tienes hermanos, ¿a qué escuela van tus amigos?

_____

G **Tareas** Tell what each person has to do for his or her class. Use **mi, tu,** or **su.**

1. Carlos tiene que preparar un informe para _____ clase de inglés.

2. Yo tengo que escribir una composición para _____ clase de inglés.

3. Juan y Lupe tienen que preparar una conversación para _____ clase de español.

4. Tú tienes que resolver cuatro problemas para _____ clase de álgebra.

5. Elena tiene que escribir a _____ tía.

H **Los primos** Tell about your cousins.

1. _____ primos viven en _____.

2. _____ casa está en la calle _____.

3. Su madre es _____ tía Dolores.

4. _____ tía Dolores, _____ madre, tiene una tienda.

5. En _____ tienda ella vende discos y videos.

I **Nuestra familia** Rewrite the sentences, changing **mi(s)** or **tu(s)** to **nuestro(s)** or **su(s).**

1. ¿Cuántas personas hay en tu familia?

_____

2. En mi familia hay cinco personas. Somos cinco.

_____

3. ¿Viven tus abuelos en Madrid?

_____

4. No, mis abuelos viven en México.

_____

5. ¿Visitan mucho tus abuelos?

_____

Un poco màs

A   **Y tú... ¿quién eres?**   Read the **Y tú... ¿quién eres?** column that appears regularly in the Mexican magazine *Eres.*

• **Ernesto López Rodríguez (15 años).**
Administración Urbana #81, Col. Ajusco, México, D.F., C.P. 04300.
Pasatiempos: leer, escribir, escuchar música y coleccionar timbres y postales.

• **Mauricio Ruiz Esparza Muñoz (15 años).**
Dr. Pedro de Alba #542, Col. San Marcos, Aguascalientes, Ags., C.P. 20070.
Pasatiempos: jugar futbol, leer Eres, ver televisión y escuchar música.

• **Mónica Lara Téllez (15 años).**
Mariano Avila #605, Int. 5, Col. Tequis, San Luis Potosí, S.L.P., C.P. 78250.
Pasatiempos: patinar, jugar hockey y escuchar música en inglés.

• **Diana Calderón Sánchez (15 años).**
Cuauhtémoc #97, Col. Del Valle, Tuxpan, Ver., C.P. 92875.
Pasatiempos: hacer gimnasia, leer Eres y coleccionar todo lo relacionado con Magneto.

• **Luis Fernando Cantú García (15 años).**
Morelos #707, Col. Zona Centro, Monclova, Coah., C.P. 25700.
Pasatiempos: ver televisión y escuchar música.

• **A. Laura Hernández (16 años).**
Vía Santa Ana #406, Fracc. Villas de Santa Ana, Monclova, Coah., C.P. 25710.
Pasatiempos: leer Eres, hablar por teléfono, escuchar música y coleccionar todo lo relacionado con Cristian Castro.

• **Eva Beatriz Rubio López (16 años).**
Tula #1129, C.F.E., Irapuato, Gto., C.P. 36361.
Pasatiempos: escuchar música, ver televisión, hacer ejercicio e ir al cine.

• **Jessica Berenice Estrada Avilés (16 años).**
José García Rdz. #2018, Col. Asturias, Monclova, Coah., C.P. 25790.
Pasatiempos: leer Eres, escuchar música y salir a pasear.

• **Cynthia Ivonne Chao Alcaraz (16 años).**
Calle 31-D #5, Col. Camarones II, Cd. del Carmen, Camp., C.P. 86130.
Pasatiempos: escuchar música, cantar, bailar, pasear y hacer cosas nuevas.

• **Blanca Fabiola y Arturo Lugo Belmonte (16 y 22 años).**
Cocotero #119, Col. Arboledas, León, Gto., C.P. 37480.
Pasatiempos: leer cómics, escuchar a Barrio Boyz y tener amigos.

• **Alejandra Alvarez Lemus (17 años).**
And. Argentina #238, Col. Aníbal Ponce, Las Guacamayas, Mich., C.P. 60990.
Pasatiempos: leer, escribir cartas, caminar y nadar.

• **Cristina Pérez Sánchez (17 años).**
5 de Mayo #10, Atengo, Jalisco, C.P. 48190.
Pasatiempos: escuchar música, leer Eres y coleccionar todo lo relacionado con Magneto.

• **Mildred Gabriela Gómez Martínez (17 años).**
Hidalgo #1759 Nte., Col. República, Saltillo, Coah., C.P. 25280.
Pasatiempos: leer, escuchar música, bailar y coleccionar todo lo relacionado con Ricky Martin.

• **Bárbara Elizabeth Vázquez Cadena (17 años).**
Francisco Sarabia #15, Col. Rosa María, Tuxpan, Ver., C.P. 92860.
Pasatiempos: leer y dibujar.

• **Jesús Alberto García (17 años).**
Calle 8a. #1408, Col. Emiliano Zapata, Cd. Ojinaga, Chih., C.P. 32881.
Pasatiempos: coleccionar Eres y todo lo relacionado con Mónica Naranjo, escuchar música y escribir cartas.

• **Giovanna Esmeralda Pérez Quijano (18 años).**
Mar del Norte #177, Fracc., Costa Verde, Boca del Río, Veracruz, C.P. 94294.
Pasatiempos: navegar por Internet, leer Eres y todo lo que tenga que ver con el WEB y escuchar música de Spice Girls

• **Liliana Gpe. Silva (20 años).**
Apdo. Postal #1928, Monterrey, N.L., C.P. 64000.
Pasatiempos: leer Eres y coleccionar todo lo relacionado con Enrique Iglesias.

• **Ma. Antonieta Caballero Espinosa (20 años).**
Prol. Paseo de la Asunción #515, Fracc. Villas del Oeste, Aguascalientes, Ags., C.P. 20280.
Pasatiempos: ir al cine, escribir y nadar.

Ma. Teresa Razo Rangel (24 años).
Ote. 15 #184, Col. Reforma, Cd. Nezahualcóyotl, Edo. de Méx., C.P. 57840.
Pasatiempos: escuchar música, jugar basquetbol, hacer aeróbics y tener amigos por correspondencia.

Jesús Argos Galván Hernández (25 años).
Pedro Fuentes #338, Fracc. Urdiñola, Saltillo, Coah., C.P. 25315.
Pasatiempos: escribir cartas e intercambiar correspondencia.

• **Gustavo Cortez (17 años).**
133 Deanna Dr., San Juan, TX., 78589, U.S.A.
Pasatiempos: patinar, coleccionar fotos de Fey, ir a conciertos y escuchar música.

• **Yina Guerrero (15 años).**
Calle 4 #4, Vilia Margarita, La Vega, Rep. Dominicana.
Pasatiempos: escuchar música, escribir cartas, coleccionar revistas, pósters y todo lo relacionado con Ricky Martin, Menudo y Magneto.

• **Roxana Funes (22 años).**
Calle 31 #640, General Pico, La Pampa, Argrgentina, C.P. 6360.
Pasatiempos: tener amigos por correspondencia y escuchar música.

• **Carolina Linares Ferrandiz (23 años).**
Apdo. Postal #405, 03500 Benidorm, Alicante, España.
Pasatiempos: coleccionar todo lo relacionado con Luis Miguel, leer, escribir, ir al cine, pintar y escuchar música.

B **Ernesto López Rodríguez** Answer the questions about Ernesto López Rodríguez according to the information in Activity A.

1. ¿Dónde vive Ernesto?

_____

2. ¿Cuántos años tiene?

_____

3. ¿Cuál es su zona postal?

_____

4. ¿Lee mucho Ernesto?

_____

5. ¿Escribe mucho también?

_____

6. ¿Qué escucha?

_____

7. ¿Qué colecciona?

_____

C **¿Quién es?** Write the name of the person(s) being described according to the information in Activity A.

1. Escuchan la música del grupo (conjunto) Barrio Boyz.

_____

2. Escucha música en inglés.

_____

3. Escribe(n) cartas.

_____

_____

4. Leen cómicos.

_____

5. Vive en Jalisco.

_____

6. Lee(n) la revista *Eres.*

_____

_____

_____

7. Ve(n) televisión.

_____

_____

_____

D   **Para vender** Read the ad that appeared in a newspaper in Puerto Rico.

SE VENDE
Dálmata de
Mes y Medio
Tel. 761-7335

E   **A escoger** Choose the word that best completes the sentence according to the information in the ad in Activity D.

Un Dálmata es _____.

   a. un teléfono

   b. un perro

   c. un gato

F   **Preguntas** Answer the questions according to the information in the ad in Activity D.

1. ¿Qué van a vender? _____

2. ¿De qué raza es el perro? _____

3. ¿Cuántos años o meses tiene el perrito? _____

4. Si vas a comprar el perro, ¿qué número de teléfono tienes que llamar? _____

Nombre _____ Fecha _____

G   **Un anuncio**   Read the ad for furniture that appeared in a newspaper in Puerto Rico.

TELEVISOR A COLOR

¡PRECIOS POR DEBAJO DE NUESTROS ESPECIALES!

19" Control remoto.
Mod. DTQ20
Reg. $266.00

ESP. **$189⁹⁵**

JUEGO DE SALA
Sofá, butaca y mecedora
Mod. 5000.
Reg. $400.00

ESP. **$279⁹⁵**

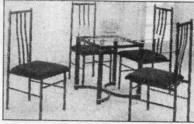

JUEGO DE COMEDOR
Mesa con 4 sillas.
Mod. 4411.
Reg. $159.00

ESP. **$99⁹⁵**

NEVERA MARCA RECONOCIDA

7.9 PIES CÚBICOS.
1 Puerta
Mod. RMC090.
Reg. $454.00

ESP. **$299⁹⁵**

65TH.INFANTERIA	ARECIBO	BAYAMON	CABO ROJO	CAGUAS	DORADO	FAJARDO	HUMACAO	HATO REY	ISABELA	PONCE	RIO GRANDE	RIO PIEDRAS
Ave. 65 de Infantería Km.4, Hills Brothers Río Piedras	Lloréns Torres 201 (frente Unidad de Salud Pública)	Carr. #2, Marginal C-17 Frente al Santa Rosa Shopping Center, Bayamón	Cabo Rojo Plaza Carr. #100, Km. 7.2	Corr. 156 Esq. Betances, Km. 60.1 Salida Aguas Buenas	Parqué Industrial Dorado Carr. Est. #693	Carr. #3 Km. 44.4 (al lado de la Cooperativa Roosevelt Road)	Calle Doctor Vidal #53 (Antiguo Teatro)	Ave. Ponce de León 452 Pda. 35 al lado de la Asociación de Maestros	Carr. #2 Int. 494 Plaza Isabela Shopping Center	Valle Real Shopping Center Ponce by pass	Carr. #3 (65th.Inf.) Km.23.5 Urb. Industrial Las Flores	De Diego #268 Casi esquina Barbosa
759-7199 759-8379	880-2778 880-2797	786-7123 740-4104	255-2210 255-2215	743-6167 743-6166	278-1028 278-1056	863-0030 863-0128	852-6875 852-6879	756-7485 756-7441	830-1188 830-0570	843-7050 843-7090	887-1130 887-1150	250-0289 250-0293

NO LAY AWAYS. *Sujeto a aprobación de crédito. 5 de cada uno de los artículos por tienda. Mensualidades para 36 meses computándose en base a 20% de pronto. Seguros de vida y propiedad (opcional) (APR21%). Precios regulares desde $20.00 a $2,000.00. Descuentos desde un 10% hasta un 50%. **Debe ser de igual marca y modelo en ventas al contado solamente. Compras financiadas sólo de $350 en adelante. NO LAY AWAYS. Oferta válida hasta el 21 de febrero.

H   **Buscando informes**   Answer the questions according to the information in the ads in Activity G.

1. ¿Cuál es el precio del televisor a color? _____

2. ¿Tiene el televisor control remoto? _____

3. ¿Cuántas mesas hay en el juego de comedor? _____

4. ¿Cuántas sillas tiene el juego? _____

5. ¿Es para la cocina o para el comedor una nevera? _____

6. ¿Cuántas puertas tiene la nevera? _____

I   **¿Cómo se dice... ?**   Find the equivalent Spanish expressions in the ad in Activity G.

1. living room set _____

2. sofa _____

3. armchair _____

4. rocker _____

Mi autobiografía

Write as much as you can about your family and your house. If you have a pet, be sure to mention him or her. Give the name and age of each of the members of your family. Then give a brief description of each one. Tell some of the activities you do at home.

Mi autobiografía

Capítulo 7
Deportes de equipo

Vocabulario   PALABRAS 1

A **El cuerpo** Identify each part of the body.

1. _____

2. _____

3. _____

4. _____

5. _____

6. _____

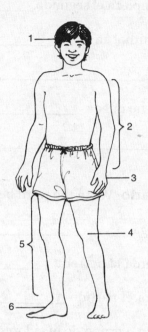

B **¿Qué es?** Identify each item.

   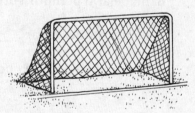

1. _____   2. _____   3. _____

4. _____   5. _____

C **Un partido de fútbol** Complete each sentence with the appropriate word.

1. Cuando juegan al fútbol, los jugadores no pueden tocar el balón con

_____.

2. Para marcar un tanto el balón tiene que entrar en la _____.

3. Cuando empieza el segundo _____, los jugadores vuelven al campo.

4. Juegan al fútbol en el _____ de fútbol.

5. El jugador _____ un tanto cuando _____ un gol.

6. Si el tanto no queda _____, un equipo gana el partido y el otro

equipo _____.

D **Un diccionario** Write the word being defined.

1. el que juega _____

2. el que guarda la portería _____

3. el que mira el partido _____

4. el conjunto o grupo de jugadores _____

5. ser victorioso _____

6. no dejar o permitir entrar _____

7. contrario de ganar _____

8. meter el balón en la portería _____

Vocabulario   PALABRAS 2

E **Deportes** Answer.

1. Write the names of three sports.

_____

2. Write four words associated with basketball.

_____

3. Write four words associated with baseball.

_____

F **Un partido de béisbol** Answer.

1. ¿Cuántas entradas hay en un partido de béisbol?

_____

2. ¿Quién lanza la pelota al bateador?

_____

3. ¿Quién batea?

_____

4. ¿Cuántas bases hay en el béisbol?

_____

5. ¿Con qué atrapa la pelota el jugador de béisbol?

_____

G **Mi deporte favorito** Write a paragraph about your favorite sport.

_____

_____

_____

_____

_____

Estructura

Verbos de cambio radical e → ie en el presente

A **¿Jugar qué?** Rewrite the following sentences in the singular.

1. Queremos jugar (al) béisbol.

_____

2. Preferimos jugar en el parque.

_____

3. Empezamos a jugar a las dos y media.

_____

4. Mis hermanos quieren jugar al fútbol.

_____

5. Ellos prefieren jugar en el campo de la escuela.

_____

6. Empiezan a jugar al mediodía.

_____

B **Al café** Rewrite the following sentences in the plural (**nosotros**).

1. Quiero comer.

_____

2. Prefiero ir al café Gijón.

_____

3. Quiero un sándwich (un bocadillo).

_____

4. Empiezo a comer.

_____

Nombre _____ Fecha _____

C **El partido de hoy** Complete each sentence with the correct form of the verb(s) in parentheses.

1. Hoy nosotros _____ a jugar a las dos. (empezar)

2. Nosotros _____ ganar. No _____ perder.
(querer, querer)

3. Si nosotros _____ el partido de hoy, _____ todo.
(perder, perder)

D **El partido de hoy** Rewrite each sentence in Activity C, changing **nosotros** to **yo**.

1. _____

2. _____

3. _____

Verbos de cambio radical **o → ue** en el presente

E **Cosas personales** Complete each sentence with the correct form of the verb in parentheses.

1. Yo _____ ocho horas cada noche. (dormir)

2. Yo _____ llegar a la escuela a las ocho menos cuarto. (poder)

3. Yo _____ tomar el autobús. (poder)

4. Yo _____ al fútbol después de las clases. (jugar)

5. Yo _____ con el equipo de la escuela. (jugar)

6. Yo _____ a casa a las cinco y media o a las seis. (volver)

7. Yo _____ muy bien después de jugar mucho. (dormir)

F   **El plural** Rewrite the sentences in Activity E, changing **yo** to **nosotros**.

1. _____

2. _____

3. _____

4. _____

5. _____

6. _____

7. _____

G   **Frases originales** Make up sentences by combining the words in each of the following columns.

Yo	querer	jugar al fútbol
Nosotros	preferir	ganar
Ellos	empezar a	perder
	poder	volver al campo
	tener que	batear
		lanzar al balón

1. _____

2. _____

3. _____

4. _____

5. _____

6. _____

WORKBOOK

Interesar, aburrir y gustar

H **Intereses y gustos** Complete each word.

1. Me gust_____ la carne pero no me gust_____ el pescado y el marisco.

2. Me gust_____ las frutas pero no me gust_____ los vegetales.

3. ¿Qué tal te gust_____ la hamburguesa?

4. Mucho. Pero no me gust_____ las papas fritas.

5. ¿Te interes_____ un postre?

I **Intereses** Write five complete sentences about things that interest you.

1. _____

2. _____

3. _____

4. _____

5. _____

J **Cosas aburridas** Write five complete sentences about things that bore you.

1. _____

2. _____

3. _____

4. _____

5. _____

K **Gustos** Write five complete sentences about things that you like.

1. _____

2. _____

3. _____

4. _____

5. _____

L **No me gusta.** Write five complete sentences about things that you do not like.

1. _____

2. _____

3. _____

4. _____

5. _____

M **Conversación** Complete the following conversation.

—Jorge, ¿ _____ gusta la historia?
           1

—Sí, _____ gusta mucho. Es el curso que más _____ interesa.
       2   3

—¿Sí? _____ sorprende. La historia _____ aburre un poco.
        4   5

—Paco, es increíble. La historia antigua _____ fascina: la historia de Roma, de Grecia, de
                                            6
Egipto.

—Pues, _____ gustan más las ciencias y las matemáticas.
         7

Un poco màs

A **Deportes** Look at the ad about sports.

DEPORTES

FÚTBOL

Los siguientes partidos de FÚTBOL corresponden a la Liga Nacional de Primera División.
Se recomienda consulten fechas por posibles cambios de fechas. / Please check dates for any changes.

• **ESTADIO SANTIAGO BERNABÉU**
P.º DE LA CASTELLANA, 104.
TEL.: 91 344 00 52. (METRO: SANTIAGO BERNABÉU).

4 Oct.
Real Madrid - Tenerife.

25 Oct.
Real Madrid - Racing.

• **ESTADIO VICENTE CALDERÓN**
VIRGEN DEL PUERTO, 67.
TEL.: 91 366 47 07. (METRO: PIRÁMIDES Y MARQUÉS DE VADILLO).

18 Oct.
Atlético de Madrid - Tenerife.

B **¿Sí o no?** Indicate whether each statement is true or false according to the ad in Activity A. If it is false correct it.

1. El Real Madrid juega contra Tenerife el 18 de octubre.

_____

2. El número de teléfono del Estadio Bernabéu es 91 344 00 52.

_____

3. El Real Madrid es un equipo de baloncesto.

_____

4. La parada de metro para el Estadio Vicente Calderón es Santiago Bernabéu.

_____

Nombre _____ Fecha _____

C **Un partido de fútbol** Read the following article about a game played in La Paz, Bolivia. The article appeared in the Bolivian newspaper *El Diario.*

> ## En 30 minutos se definió el partido
>
> Con goles convertidos por Etcheverry, Borja y Baldivieso en el transcurso de 30 minutos del segundo período, el plantel de Bolívar se impuso a Cobreloa de Chile por 3 a 0, en partido válido para la Copa Libertadores de América, anoche en el estadio Olímpico de Miraflores ante más de 36.000 espectadores.

D **Preguntas** In a word or two, answer the following questions (in English) about the article in Activity C.

1. What is the article about? _____

2. Who scored the goals? _____

3. When did all the scoring take place? _____

4. What was the final score? _____

E **Información** Find the following information in the article in Activity C.

1. el nombre del estadio _____

2. el país que Cobreloa representa _____

3. el número de espectadores en el estadio _____

Nombre _____ Fecha _____

 El tenis Read the following article that appeared in the magazine *Vanidades.*

El origen del tenis

La palabra «tenis» — aplicada al popular deporte — viene del árabe «tenetz», una adaptación de la palabra «tenez» que significa «saltar». Y la palabra «raqueta» viene también del árabe, ya que «rahet» significa «en la palma de la mano» y cuando el deporte se inició, los jugadores le daban a la pelota usando la palma de la mano en vez de utilizar una raqueta, como en nuestros días.

G **Preguntas** In a word or two, answer the following questions about the article in Activity A.

1. ¿Qué es el tenis?

_____

2. ¿De qué lengua viene la palabra «tenis»?

_____

3. ¿Viene la palabra «raqueta» de la misma lengua?

_____

4. Hoy, ¿usan los tenistas la palma de la mano para darle a la pelota?

_____

5. En vez de usar la palma de la mano, ¿qué usan o utilizan?

_____

Mi autobiografía

Write as much as you can about the sports teams at your school. Do you participate in any team sports? Do you prefer to participate or to be a spectator? If you are not fond of sports, write about some of your other activities.

Mi autobiografía

CHECK-UP 2

A Identify each of the following.

1. _____

2. _____

3. _____

4. _____

5. _____

6. _____

7. _____

8. _____

9. _____

WORKBOOK
Copyright © by The McGraw-Hill Companies, Inc.

¡Buen viaje! Level 1 Check-Up 2   83

B Complete each sentence with the appropriate word(s).

1. Dos cuartos de una casa son _____ y _____.

2. La familia vive en una _____ particular, no en un apartamento.

3. Ellos viven en la _____ Main.

4. María _____ un sándwich y _____ una limonada.

5. Yo leo el _____ y escribo con un _____.

6. Alrededor de la casa hay un _____.

7. Yo tengo una bicicleta y mis padres tienen un _____ en el garaje.

8. El fútbol y el béisbol son _____.

9. Juegan al fútbol en el _____ de fútbol.

10. Si el _____ no puede parar el balón y el balón entra en la portería, el

    otro _____ mete un gol y marca un _____.

C Complete each sentence with the correct form of the verb in parentheses.

1. Yo _____ la televisión en la sala. (ver)

2. Nosotros _____ en el comedor. (comer)

3. Nosotros _____ en una casa particular. (vivir)

4. Yo _____ notas muy buenas en la escuela. (recibir)

5. Ellos _____ mucho. (leer)

6. Yo _____ una familia grande. (tener)

7. Nosotros _____ un perro. (tener)

8. Mi tía _____ tres hijos. (tener)

9. Yo _____ jugar con ellos. (preferir)

10. El portero no _____ bloquear el balón. (poder)

11. Ellos _____ bien después de un partido. (dormir)

12. Nosotros _____ ganar el partido. (querer)

D Rewrite each sentence, changing the singular to the plural or vice versa.

1. Yo empiezo ahora.

Nosotros _____.

2. Él quiere lanzar la pelota.

Ellos _____.

3. ¿Tú puedes?

¿Ustedes _____?

4. Ellos juegan bien.

Él _____.

5. Yo vuelvo ahora.

Nosotros _____.

6. Yo prefiero comer ahora.

Nosotros _____.

7. Ellas duermen ocho horas.

Ella _____.

E Complete each sentence with the correct form of the possessive adjective(s).

1. Yo tengo una hermana. _____ hermana tiene once años.

2. El libro es de Juan. _____ libro es muy interesante.

3. Nosotros vivimos en los suburbios. _____ casa tiene un jardín.

4. Mi tío es muy simpático. _____ hijos son _____ primos.

5. Si vas a jugar al béisbol, ¿tienes _____ bate y _____ guante?

WORKBOOK
Copyright © by The McGraw-Hill Companies, Inc.

¡Buen viaje! Level 1 Check-Up 2   **85**

F Complete each sentence with **tener que** or **ir a.**

1. En el juego de béisbol, el pícher _____ lanzar la pelota al bateador.

2. Yo _____ estudiar mucho si quiero recibir buenas notas.

3. Mañana nosotros _____ tener un examen. Nosotros

_____ estudiar para el examen.

4. Elena y Paco _____ ir a la tienda de discos. Ellos

_____ comprar un regalo para su prima, Teresa. Teresa

_____ cumplir los quince años el martes.

G Tell whether each statement is true or false. Write **sí** or **no.**

_____ **1.** En los países hispanos los jóvenes van a un café con sus amigos.

_____ **2.** Venden productos congelados en un mercado al aire libre.

_____ **3.** En los países hispanos dan una fiesta en honor de un muchacho que cumple los quince años.

_____ **4.** Cuando un joven hispano habla de su familia, sólo habla de sus padres y sus hermanos.

_____ **5.** En Latinoamérica hay muchos equipos nacionales de fútbol. Por ejemplo, Perú tiene su equipo, Argentina tiene su equipo, etc.

Capítulo 8
La salud y el médico

Vocabulario   PALABRAS 1

A **¿Cómo está la persona?** Describe each person's condition according to the illustration.

1. _____

2. _____

3. _____

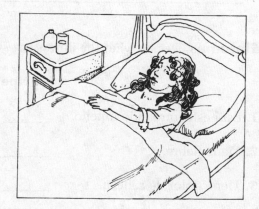

4. _____

B **De otra manera** Express each of the following in a different way.

1. Ella *tiene catarro*.

_____

2. Él *tose mucho*.

_____

3. Tiene *la temperatura elevada*.

_____

4. *Me duele* la cabeza.

_____

5. *Me duele* el estómago.

_____

6. Estoy *melancólico*.

_____

7. El enfermo tiene que *pasar mucho tiempo en cama*.

_____

C **Síntomas** Decide what the illness is.

	la gripe	un catarro	los dos
1. Está estornudando mucho.	_____	_____	_____
2. Tiene fiebre.	_____	_____	_____
3. Tiene dolor de cabeza.	_____	_____	_____
4. Tiene tos.	_____	_____	_____
5. Tiene escalofríos.	_____	_____	_____

Vocabulario PALABRAS 2

D **¡Cuánto me duele!** Tell where it hurts according to the illustration.

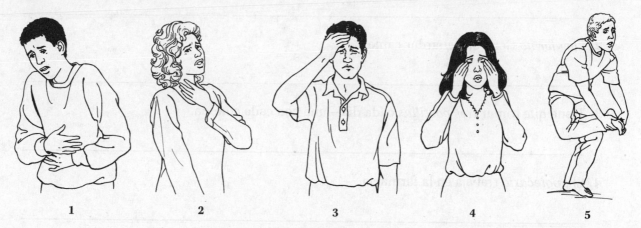

1   2   3   4   5

1. _____

2. _____

3. _____

4. _____

5. _____

E **La medicina** Complete each sentence with the appropriate word(s).

1. El médico examina a sus pacientes en el _____ o en la

_____.

2. Yo abro la boca cuando el médico me examina la _____.

3. El médico me da una _____ para antibióticos.

4. Cada día tengo que tomar mis medicamentos: tres _____ o

_____.

5. El farmacéutico trabaja en la _____.

6. El farmacéutico o la farmacéutica _____ los medicamentos.

F **De otra manera** Express each of the following in a different way.

1. El enfermo está con el médico en su *consultorio.*

_____

2. *El enfermo* tiene que guardar cama.

_____

3. Tiene que tomar tres *pastillas* cada día—una con cada comida.

_____

4. El *apotecario* trabaja en la farmacia.

_____

5. La farmacéutica *vende* los medicamentos.

_____

G **La salud** Complete each sentence with the appropriate word.

aspirina   síntomas   diagnosis

antibióticos   alergia   dosis

1. Estornudo mucho porque tengo una _____ a los gatos.

2. Pablo tiene dolor de cabeza. Tiene que tomar _____.

3. El médico me receta unos _____ porque tengo la gripe.

4. Elena está enferma. Tiene muchas _____: estornuda, tiene tos, tiene fiebre y escalofríos y también tiene dolor de garganta.

5. La _____ es tres píldoras cada día.

6. Según el médico, la _____ es la gripe asiática.

Estructura

Ser y estar

A   **¿Cómo es o cómo está?** Write sentences, using words from each column.

Felipe	es	muy inteligente
Gloria	está	simpático
		serio
		nervioso
		enfermo
		contento
		triste

1. _____

2. _____

3. _____

4. _____

5. _____

6. _____

7. _____

B   **¿De dónde es? ¿Dónde está?** Look at the maps. The first map tells where the person is from. The second map tells where the person is right now. Write a sentence telling where the person is from and where he/she is now. Use **ser** and **estar**.

ESTADOS UNIDOS   ESPAÑA

1. Yo _____

_____

2. Alberto y Lola _____

_____

3. Isabel _____

_____

4. Nosotros _____

_____

C **¿Y tú?** Give your own answers.

1. ¿De dónde eres? ¿Dónde estás ahora?

_____

_____

2. Tu mamá o tu papá, ¿de dónde es? ¿Dónde está ahora?

_____

_____

D **La médica** Complete with the correct forms of **ser** or **estar**.

La médica _____ muy inteligente. Ella _____ de Nicaragua.
                    1   2

_____ nicaragüense. Ella _____ especialista en cirugía.
        3   4

_____ cirujana. Muchos de sus pacientes _____ muy
        5   6

enfermos. Pero la doctora García _____ muy simpática. Ella
                                         7

_____ muy amable con sus pacientes. Su consultorio _____
        8   9

en el hospital mismo. _____ en la planta baja del hospital. La sala de
                              10

operaciones _____ en el mismo edificio que su consultorio.
                    11

Me, te, nos

E **Al médico** Answer the following questions.

1. Si estás enfermo(a), ¿te examina el médico?

_____

2. ¿Te da la diagnosis?

_____

3. Si tienes dolor de garganta, ¿te receta unas pastillas el médico?

_____

4. Carlos, ¿me va a dar una inyección el médico?

_____

F **En la consulta del médico** Complete the conversation.

—José, ¿dónde _____ duele?
                      1

—Ay, doctor. _____ duele en todas partes. _____ duele la cabeza, _____ duele la garganta.
                      2   3   4

—Muy bien, José. _____ voy a examinar. ¿ _____ permites?
                          5   6

Un poco màs

A **Ejercicios** Read the directions for some exercises that will relieve stress.

Ejercicios contra el estrés

1 Sentada en el suelo, con las piernas cruzadas y la espalda recta, lleva los brazos atrás con las manos unidas y estíralos diez veces.

2 En cuclillas, con las manos apoyadas sobre el suelo, lleva una pierna hacia atrás. Cambia de pierna diez veces.

3 Sentada, pon una pierna recta y la otra flexionada por encima. Cambia diez veces de pierna.

B **Expresiones** Read the directions again and look for the Spanish equivalents of the following expressions.

1. seated on the floor _____

2. back straight _____

3. squatting _____

4. legs crossed _____

5. hands on the floor _____

6. one leg straight and the other bent _____

C **Ahora en inglés** Rewrite the directions for the exercises in Activity A in English.

1. _____

_____

2. _____

_____

3. _____

_____

D **La Asociación Betel** Read the flyer prepared by Asociación Betel, an organization that helps people in need. To understand the flyer it is necessary to know the meaning of the word **muebles: Las sillas, las mesas y las camas son muebles.**

¿Quiere comprar muebles
a precios muy bajos?

¿Quiere ayudar a personas que
están dejando la droga?

¿No sabe qué hacer con sus
muebles viejos o usados?

¡Ya sabe la solución!
¡LLAME AL RASTRO BETEL!

RECOGEMOS Y VENDEMOS:

☑ MUEBLES DE TODO TIPO
☑ ELECTRODOMÉSTICOS
☑ ANTIGÜEDADES
☑ COCHES USADOS
☑ ROPA USADA

RESTAURAMOS MUEBLES

HACEMOS TAPICERÍA

*TODO beneficio en favor del Centro
de Rehabilitación de Marginados*

El Rastro BETEL más cerca de Vd. está en:
Avda. Ajalvir a Vicálvaro, 43
CANILLEJAS
☎ **320 24 84**

Metro Torre Arias (línea 5)
C/ Alcalá
BETEL
Cuartel Militar — Rastro e Ingresos IGLESIA
Avda. Arcentales

ASOCIACIÓN BETEL
Ofreciendo una Salida al Marginado

E **A escoger** Choose the correct completion for each sentence.

1. El rastro es _____.

   a. un mercado grande donde venden artículos nuevos a precios altos
   b. un mercado donde venden cosas viejas y usadas a precios muy bajos
   c. una tienda elegante

2. Los marginados son _____.

   a. personas que restauran muebles
   b. personas con problemas sociales que necesitan ayuda o rehabilitación
   c. personas que trabajan con la Asociación Betel

F **Preguntas** Answer according to the information in the flyer in Activity D.

1. ¿Qué vende la Asociación Betel en el rastro Betel? _____

_____

2. ¿A quiénes ayuda y rehabilita la Asociación Betel? _____

_____

G **Devoradores de pescado** Read the following chart.

Devoradores de pescado

España es el cuarto país del mundo en consumo de pescado, por detrás de Islandia, Japón y Portugal.

PESCADO EN LA DIETA (KILOS POR PERSONA Y AÑO)

ISLANDIA	138
JAPÓN	75
PORTUGAL	49
ESPAÑA	39
FRANCIA	31
GRECIA	28
SUECIA	28
ESTADOS UNIDOS	22
ITALIA	21
ALEMANIA	20
REINO UNIDO	19
IRLANDA	17
HOLANDA	10

H **Buscando informes** Answer according to the information in the chart in Activity G.

1. Es bueno para la salud comer mucho pescado y poca carne roja. ¿Cuántos kilos de

   pescado come un español en un año? _____

2. ¿En cuántos países consumen más (+) pescado que en España? _____

3. ¿En cuántos países consumen menos (-) pescado que en España? _____

4. ¿Cuántos kilos de pescado consume en un año un individuo en Estados Unidos?

   _____

Nombre _____ Fecha _____

I   **Una notificación** Read the following notice.

El **Dr. Enrique Segura**
Tiene el placer de notificarles a sus
pacientes, colegas y amigos el
traslado de su práctica de
Obstetricia y Ginecología a la

Suite 408
Edificio Arturo Cadilla
Hospital San Pablo
Tels. 740-8116 - 787-1060

J   **Preguntas** Answer according to the information in the notice in Activity I.

1. ¿Quién es el médico?

_____

2. ¿Para quiénes es la notificación?

_____

3. ¿Dónde está su nuevo consultorio?

_____

4. ¿En qué hospital trabaja el médico?

_____

Mi autobiografía

Tell some things about yourself. What makes you happy? What makes you sad? What do you do when you don't feel well? What is the name of your family doctor? Write about some of the minor ailments you get once in a while. Are you a good patient or not? You may want to ask a family member for an opinion.

Mi autobiografía

WORKBOOK

Capítulo 9
El verano y el invierno

Vocabulario   PALABRAS 1

A ¿Qué es? Identify each item.

1. _____

2. _____

3. _____

4. _____

5. _____   6. _____

7. _____   8. _____

B **El verano** Answer with as complete a description as possible.

¿Qué tiempo hace en el verano?

_____

_____

_____

_____

_____

_____

_____

_____

Nombre _____ Fecha _____

C **En la playa** Match the activity with the illustration.

a

b

c

d

e

f

1. _____ nadar

2. _____ bucear

3. _____ practicar la plancha de vela

4. _____ esquiar en el agua

5. _____ tomar el sol

6. _____ practicar la tabla hawaiana

D   **Una tarjeta postal** Read Eduardo's postcard. Then answer the questions that follow.

Queridos amigos,

Aquí estoy en la playa de
Marbella. Marbella es un pueblo
bonito en la Costa del Sol, en
el sur de España. El mar
aquí, el Mediterráneo, siempre
está en calma en el verano.
A veces hay algunas olas
pequeñas. Todos los días
hace buen tiempo. Siempre
uso una crema protectora.
¡Qué contento estoy aquí!

Saludos, Eduardo

La Familia Salas
Calle Sol, No. 4
San Juan, PR
00926

1. ¿Dónde está Eduardo?

_____

2. ¿Dónde está Marbella?

_____

3. ¿Marbella está en la Costa del Sol?

_____

4. ¿Cómo está el mar Mediterráneo, sobre todo en el verano?

_____

5. A veces, ¿qué hay en el mar?

_____

6. ¿Qué usa Eduardo?

_____

E   **El tenis** Complete the paragraph according to the illustration.

Cada jugador de tenis tiene su _____. Juegan _____,
                                          1   **2**

no _____. Juegan en una _____, no cubierta.
          3   **4**

Cuando juegan tenis la _____ tiene que pasar por encima de la
                                          5

_____.
          6

Vocabulario   PALABRAS 2

F   **Para esquiar** Write down some things you would have to get before going skiing.

_____

_____

_____

_____

_____

G **A esquiar en el invierno** Complete each sentence with the appropriate word(s).

1. Los esquiadores suben la montaña en _____.

2. Compran los _____ para _____ en la ventanilla o

   _____.

3. José bajó la _____ para expertos.

4. Si uno va a esquiar, necesita _____, _____ y

   _____.

5. En el invierno hace _____.

6. A veces, la temperatura _____ a cinco grados bajo cero.

H **El invierno** Answer with as complete a description as possible.

¿Qué tiempo hace en el invierno?

_____

_____

_____

_____

_____

I **Palabras derivadas** Match each verb in the left-hand column with the corresponding noun in the right-hand column.

1. _____ subir   **a.** el esquí

2. _____ bajar   **b.** la nieve, la nevada

3. _____ descender   **c.** la bajada

4. _____ esquiar   **d.** la subida

5. _____ nevar   **e.** el descenso

Estructura

Pretérito de los verbos en -ar

A **El verano** Complete each sentence with the correct preterite forms of the verb in parentheses.

1. Él _____ en el mar y yo _____ en el lago. (esquiar)

2. Ella _____ en el lago y yo _____ en la piscina. (nadar)

3. Él _____ una crema protectora y yo _____ una crema protectora también. (usar)

B **De compras** Complete with the correct preterite forms of the verbs in parentheses.

—¿Qué _____ tú? (comprar)
          1

—_____ una raqueta. (Comprar)
   2

—¿Dónde la _____? (comprar)
         3

—La _____ en una tienda en el centro comercial. (comprar)
    4

—¿Cuánto _____? (pagar)
       5

—_____ cinco mil pesos. (Pagar)
   6

C **Una visita al museo** Rewrite each sentence in the plural.

1. Visitó el museo del Prado.

_____

2. Compró billetes reducidos para estudiantes.

_____

3. Entró en el museo.

_____

4. Miró los cuadros de Goya, Velázquez y El Greco. Admiró *Las Meninas* de Velázquez.

_____

5. Pasó unas tres horas en el museo.

_____

D **¿Y ustedes?** Complete each sentence with the correct form of the verb in parentheses.

1. (llegar)

Ayer nosotros _____ a la escuela a las ocho.

¿A qué hora _____ ustedes?

2. (hablar)

Ayer nosotros _____ con la profesora de español.

¿Con quién _____ ustedes?

3. (tomar)

Nosotros _____ un examen.

¿En qué clase lo _____ ustedes?

4. (tomar)

Nosotros _____ el almuerzo en la cafetería.

¿Dónde lo _____ ustedes?

5. (jugar)

Después de las clases, nosotros _____ al tenis.

¿Cuándo _____ ustedes?

6. (pagar)

Nosotros _____ 150 pesos por los boletos.

¿Cuánto _____ ustedes?

Nombre _____ Fecha _____

E **Un día en la playa de Marbella** Complete each sentence with the correct preterite verb ending.

1. Anita tom_____ el sol.

2. José Luis nad_____.

3. Yo esqui_____ en el agua.

4. Maripaz y Nando buce_____.

5. Y luego todos nosotros tom_____ un refresco en un café.

6. Yo tom_____ una limonada.

7. Anita tom_____ un helado.

8. ¿Y quién pag_____? Anita pag_____.

9. Y tú, ¿pas_____ el día en la playa con tus amigos?

10. ¿No? ¿Ustedes no pas_____ el día en la playa? ¡Qué pena!

F **¡Cuidado!** Complete each sentence with the correct preterite forms of the verb in parentheses.

1. Yo _____ la guitarra y él la _____ también. (tocar)

2. Yo _____ y ella _____ también. (jugar)

3. Yo _____ y él _____ a la misma hora. (llegar)

4. Yo _____ un tanto y ella _____ otro. (marcar)

5. Yo _____ y ella _____ también. (pagar)

6. Yo _____ a las ocho y él _____ a las nueve. (empezar)

7. Yo _____ una mesa libre y él _____ una mesa libre. (buscar)

Pronombres—lo, la, los, las

G **La playa** Rewrite each sentence, substituting **lo, la, los,** or **las** for the indicated direct object.

1. Teresa compró *la crema protectora.*

_____

2. Ella usó *la crema protectora* en la playa.

_____

3. Carlos tiene un nuevo bañador. Él compró *el bañador* ayer.

_____

4. Los amigos de Carlos y Teresa pasaron un día muy agradable. Pasaron *el día* en la playa.

_____

5. Ellos esquiaron en el agua. Compraron *los esquís* en una tienda cerca de la playa.

_____

6. Rafael usa anteojos de sol. Compró *los anteojos de sol* ayer.

_____

7. Yo tomé fotos instantáneas. Tomé *las fotos* en la playa.

_____

8. Carmen miró *las fotos.*

_____

H **¿Adónde vas?** Answer each question. Use object pronouns when possible.

1. ¿Tienes la raqueta? _____

¿Adónde vas? _____

2. ¿Tienes la plancha de vela? _____

¿Adónde vas? _____

3. ¿Tienes tu bañador? _____

¿Tienes los esquís acuáticos? _____

¿Qué vas a practicar? _____

4. ¿Tienes la pelota? _____

¿Tienes el bate? _____

¿Tienes el guante? _____

¿A qué vas a jugar? _____

5. ¿Tienes los esquís? _____

¿Tienes los bastones? _____

¿Tienes tus guantes? _____

¿Tienes tus botas? _____

¿Adónde vas? _____

Ir y ser en el pretérito

1 **¡Ayer!** Complete each sentence with the correct preterite forms of **ir.**

1. Yo _____ a la escuela y él también _____.

2. Yo _____ al mercado y él también _____.

3. Yo _____ a la playa y él también _____.

4. Yo _____ al lago y él también _____.

5. Nosotros _____ a la piscina y ellos también _____.

6. Nosotros _____ al campo de fútbol y ellos también

   _____.

7. Nosotros _____ a esquiar y ellos también _____.

Nombre _____ Fecha _____

Un poco màs

A **Deportes de invierno** Read the following information about winter sports that appeared in an educational journal published by the **Embajada de España.**

DEPORTES DE INVIERNO

Con el invierno llegan los deportes del frío. Es la época propicia para practicar las distintas variedades de esquí: alpino, nórdico, en monopatín, así como las carreras de trineos, el patinaje sobre hielo, el biatlón, el bob-sled...

Los Pirineos es una de las zonas de España donde mejor se pueden practicar todos estos deportes.

Blanca Fernández Ochoa ha sido la mejor esquiadora española de los últimos tiempos. Fue medalla de bronce en las últimas olimpiadas de Albertville.

El **Biatlón** es un nuevo deporte olímpico que combina el esquí y el tiro.

El **esquí-alpinismo**
Con una técnica específica es posible subir las pendientes más difíciles para luego realizar el descenso sobre nieve fresca o hielo.

El **surf de nieve**
Para practicarlo necesitas una tabla y un casco, rodilleras... Hay dos modalidades: las carreras y las exhibiciones.

Las **carreras de trineos**
El éxito de este deporte depende de la compenetración entre los perros y el deportista. Doce perros tiran del trineo.

El **bob-sled** es un deporte de gran emoción. Destreza en la conducción y una buena dosis de valor son los dos ingredientes básicos para su práctica.

Patinaje sobre hielo
Con unos patines de hielo puedes hacer maravillas: desde montar una coreografía con tu melodía favorita, hasta competir con tus amigos para ver quien es el más rápido sobre las cuchillas.

B **Expresiones** Find the Spanish equivalent for the following in the article about winter sports.

1. bronze medal _____

2. downhill skiing _____

3. cross-country skiing _____

4. helmet _____

5. knee pads _____

6. blades _____

7. snowboarding _____

El buceo Read this ad about snorkeling lessons.

Cursos de Buceo

SI TODAVIA NO ERES BUCEADOR, AHORA ES EL MOMENTO DE COMENZAR ESTA AVENTURA

- Cursos de Buceo con titulación internacional de **S.S.I.**

- Todo el material, equipamiento, tramitaciones, etc., necesario para el curso esta incluido en nuestro precio.

- Grupos reducidos.

- Diversas posibilidades para que puedas elegir la que mejor se ajuste a tus necesidades.

- Nuestros cursos destacan por el número de inmersiones que realizas en ellos.

DURANTE TODO EL AÑO impartimos curso en nuestro Centro de Buceo. Duración una semana.

DURANTE LOS PUENTES DE SEMANA SANTA Y MAYO, cursos intensivos en la Costa.

CURSOS EN MADRID. Si no puedes desplazarte a la Costa, ahora te ofrecemos el curso impartido en Madrid, en horario totalmente flexible, para que puedas compatibilizarlo con tu trabajo o estudios.

INFORMATE Y RESERVA TU PLAZA

CENTRO DE BUCEO DARDANUS

CASTELL DE FERRO (Granada)
Teléfonos: 958/656008 y 908/625822

EN MADRID
Teléfonos: 91/5173212 y 909/167559

D **Información** Answer the questions according to the information in the ad in Activity C.

1. ¿Cuándo dan los cursos de buceo?

_____

2. ¿Cuánto tiempo dura un curso?

_____

3. ¿Son grandes o pequeños los grupos que forman una clase?

_____

4. ¿Cuándo hay cursos en la Costa?

_____

E **¿Sí o no?** Indicate whether the following statements are true or false according to the information in the ad in Activity C. Write **sí** or **no**.

1. _____ Hay muchas personas en cada grupo o clase.

2. _____ Es necesario ir a la Costa para tomar el curso.

3. _____ El centro de Buceo Dardanus permite a los estudiantes tener muchas inmersiones.

4. _____ Dan cursos sólo en mayo.

5. _____ Todo lo que uno necesita para bucear está incluido en el precio.

6. _____ Las horas de los cursos son flexibles.

F **El puente** Read about a special use of the word **puente**.

In the ad for the Centro de Buceo Dardanus the word **puente** is used.

DURANTE LOS PUENTES DE SEMANA SANTA Y MAYO

This is a special use of the word puente. **Un puente** is a bridge.
   Un puente famoso en la Ciudad de Nueva York es el puente Wáshington.
   Un puente famoso de San Francisco es el puente Golden Gate.
Semana Santa and **Mayo** are two holidays in Spain that come close to one another. People will often take time off between the two close holidays to go on a short vacation. This time between the holidays is referred to as **un puente**.
   The word **puente** is also used to mean "shuttle." For example, **el puente aéreo** is the air shuttle for flights that operate every hour between Madrid and Barcelona or Buenos Aires and Montevideo.

G   **Doriance** Read the following ad.

Prepara, estimula y prolonga el bronceado.

▶ **DORIANCE** es un complemento nutricional innovador que ayuda a obtener un bonito tono dorado de la piel.

▶ **DORIANCE**, aporta al organismo una serie de sustancias naturales que facilitan el proceso natural del bronceado de la piel, pero que no protegen por sí mismas de la acción nociva de los rayos UV solares. **DORIANCE** no es un cosmético, por ello, es recomendable que la exposición al sol se realice de forma gradual y empleando una crema solar adecuada a cada tipo de piel.

▶ **DORIANCE** es muy rico en beta-caroteno y otros carotenoides naturales extraídos de un alga marina, la Dunaliella salina. El beta-caroteno (presente, por ejemplo, también en las zanahorias, tomates y otras frutas) estimula el proceso natural de pigmentación de la piel tras la exposición al sol y tiene además un efecto antioxidante.

▶ **DORIANCE** contiene también Vitaminas C y E que refuerzan las propiedades protectoras y anti-âge del beta-caroteno, así como Aceite de Borraja, rico en ácidos grasos esenciales.

▶ **DORIANCE** es adecuado para todo tipo de piel y, particularmente, para las pieles sensibles al sol que broncean con dificultad.

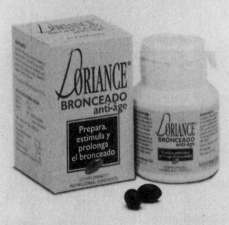

Complemento nutricional específico

Alga Dunaliella salina

H   **Una pregunta** According to the ad in Activity G there are several benefits to using Doriance. What are they? You may write your answers in English.

_____

_____

_____

_____

_____

_____

_____

_____

¡A esquiar! Read the following advertisement from an Argentine newspaper. In a word or two, answer each question according to the ad.

1. What is the name of the travel agency?

   _____

2. How many types of excursions does the travel agency offer?

   _____

3. Is it necessary to have one's own equipment in order to book a trip?

   _____

4. Are there trips for beginners as well as experts?

   _____

5. Is there only one departure each week?

   _____

6. How many departures are there each week?

   _____

7. When do the departures begin?

   _____

8. When do the departures end? _____

9. Which ski resort do these trips go to? _____

10. In what country is Portillo? _____

11. The prices shown are for how many days? _____

ESQUÍ

A NIVEL *Cavaliere*

Cavaliere, el operador turístico de nivel internacional

CUATRO CATEGORÍAS

- **Expertos con equipo**
  Incluye profesor de su nivel y provisión de equipo
- **Expertos**
  Igual cobertura, sin la provisión de equipo
- **Futuros**
  Provisión de equipo completo y dos clases diarias con profesor exclusivo para grupos reducidos
- **Niños con escuela de esquí**
  Niños de 3 a 11 años que pasan el día entero a cargo de personal especializado y aprenden jugando. Se incluye pensión completa y provisión de equipo.

CUATRO SALIDAS SEMANALES

Martes, Jueves, Sábados y Domingos

desde el 19 de junio hasta el 23 de octubre

Portillo — 8 días

Expertos c/ equipo	de 39.980 a 52.000
Expertos	de 3l.700 a 51.500
Futuros	de 40.680 a 54.900
Niños / escuela	de 32.900 a 48.300

Cavaliere

lo prometido... y más.
Córdoba 617 primer piso • Res. 658 • 74

Mi autobiografía

Write about the summer and winter weather where you live. Tell which season you prefer. Do you like both summer and winter activities? Write as much as you can about both summer and winter activities that you participate in.

Mi autobiografía

Capítulo 10
Diversiones culturales

Vocabulario   PALABRAS 1

A **En la taquilla** Complete each sentence with the appropriate word(s).

1. La gente compra sus _____ o boletos para el cine en la

   _____ .

2. Hay una _____ a las 18:30 y hay otra a las 21:30.

3. El film es popular y mucha gente quiere comprar _____ . Hay una

   _____ delante de la taquilla.

4. En el cine presentan la película en una _____ grande.

5. No quiero una _____ en la primera _____ . Está
   demasiado cerca de la pantalla y no veo bien.

B **Sinónimos** Match the word in the left-hand column with a word that means the same in
the right-hand column.

1. _____ la taquilla   **a.** la localidad, el boleto, el billete

2. _____ la entrada   **b.** la silla, el asiento

3. _____ la película   **c.** la ventanilla, la boletería

4. _____ la butaca   **d.** la fila

5. _____ la cola   **e.** el film, el filme

C **Una película** Complete each sentence with the appropriate word(s).

1. El joven _____ una película en el cine Rex.

2. No vio la película doblada. La vio en _____ con

_____ en español.

3. Él no volvió a casa en autobús. Cuando salió del cine, _____ el autobús.

4. Como perdió el bus, decidió tomar el _____.

5. Subió al metro en la _____ Insurgentes.

Vocabulario   PALABRAS 2

D **¿Quién es o qué es?** Identify each item.

1. _____   2. _____   3. _____

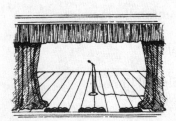

4. _____   5. _____

E **¿Quién es?** Write the profession of the person being described.

1. Él pinta cuadros.

_____

2. Ella juega el papel de un personaje en una obra teatral o en una película.

_____

3. Él escribe obras literarias.

_____

4. Él juega el papel de un personaje en una obra teatral o en una película.

_____

F **¿Sí o no?** Tell whether each statement is true or false. Write **sí** or **no.**

1. _____ Siempre hay una exposición de arte en el cine.

2. _____ Ellos ven una película en la pantalla.

3. _____ Un carro es un medio de transporte.

4. _____ La escultora dio una representación en el teatro.

5. _____ Los actores entran en el telón.

6. _____ Los espectadores aplauden después de una comedia musical si les gustó.

7. _____ Los artistas pintaron el mural.

8. _____ Antes de entrar en el teatro es necesario comprar una taquilla.

G **Unas preguntas** Make up a question about each statement. The answer to the question would be the italicized word(s).

1. Alejandra salió *anoche*.

_____

2. Ella salió con *una amiga*.

_____

3. Ellas vieron *una película* en el Cine Imperial.

_____

4. Ellos vieron una película *en el Cine Imperial*.

_____

5. Ellos pagaron *cuatro pesos* por las entradas.

_____

6. La sesión empezó *a las ocho*.

_____

7. La película fue *muy buena*.

_____

8. Ellos volvieron a casa *en el metro*.

_____

Estructura

Pretérito de los verbos en -er e -ir

 Una carta a un(a) amigo(a) Write a friend a short letter. Tell him or her: you went out last night; you saw a good movie; you saw the movie at the Cine Rex; afterwards you ate at a restaurant; you returned home at 10:30.

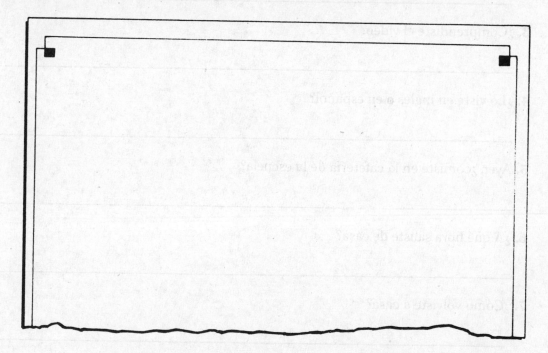

Otra carta Rewrite the letter from Activity A. Tell your friend what you and Guillermo did.

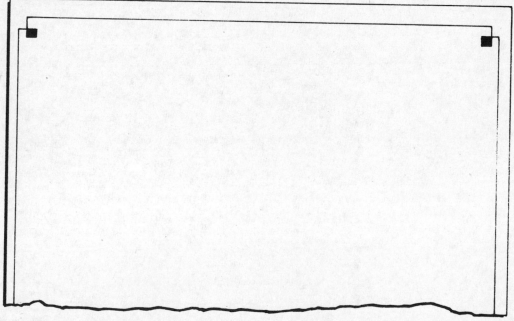

C   **Yo** Answer the following questions about yourself.

1. Ayer, ¿viste un video en la clase de español?

_____

2. ¿Aprendiste algo nuevo en clase?

_____

3. ¿Comprendiste el video?

_____

4. ¿Lo viste en inglés o en español?

_____

5. Ayer, ¿comiste en la cafetería de la escuela?

_____

6. ¿A qué hora saliste de casa?

_____

7. ¿Cómo volviste a casa?

_____

Nombre _____ Fecha _____

D   **Anoche** Complete each sentence with the correct preterite form of the verb(s) in parentheses.

1. Roberto _____ anoche y no _____ a casa hasta la medianoche. (salir, volver)

2. Él y sus amigos _____ al cine donde _____ una película. (ir, ver)

3. Ellos la _____ en inglés, en versión original. (ver)

4. Ellos la _____ sin problema. (comprender)

5. Vicente, ¿ _____ tú la película? (comprender)

6. Claro que yo la _____. _____ mucho inglés en la escuela. (comprender, Aprender)

7. Cuando nosotros _____ del café, _____ el autobús. (salir, perder)

8. ¿Cómo _____ ustedes a casa? (volver)

9. Nosotros _____ en taxi. (volver)

E   **Hoy no, ayer.** Rewrite all the sentences, changing **hoy** to **ayer.**

1. Hoy como en casa.

_____

2. Hoy vemos una película.

_____

3. ¿Qué escribes hoy para la clase de inglés?

_____

4. ¿A qué hora salen ustedes hoy?

_____

5. ¿Dan ustedes una fiesta hoy?

_____

Complementos le, les

F **La carta** Complete with **le, les, lo, la, los,** or **las.** Be careful in deciding whether you need a direct object or an indirect object.

TERESA: Esta noche _____ tengo que escribir una carta a Carmen.
                              1

ALEJANDRO: ¿ _____ tienes que escribir? ¿Por qué?
            2

TERESA: ¿Pues, yo recibí una carta de ella.

ALEJANDRO: ¿Ah, sí? ¿Cuándo _____ recibiste?
                       3

TERESA: _____ recibí la semana pasada.
       4

ALEJANDRO: Pues, sí. Es verdad que _____ tienes que escribir. ¿Qué _____ vas a decir?
                                      5   6

TERESA: _____ tengo que decir que no puedo asistir a su fiesta.
       7

ALEJANDRO: ¿A su fiesta?

TERESA: Sí, sus padres _____ van a dar una fiesta en honor del día de su santo.
                             8

ALEJANDRO: ¿ _____ escribiste a sus padres también?
            9

TERESA: No. ¿Por qué me preguntas?

ALEJANDRO: Pues, si no puedes asistir a la fiesta, _____ debes presentar tus excusas a sus
                                                  10
padres también.

TERESA: Tienes razón. Luego _____ voy a escribir una carta a Carmen y _____ voy a
                                    11   12

escribir otra a sus padres.

G **Los complementos** Rewrite each sentence, substituting a pronoun for the indicated object.

1. Ellos vieron *la película* en el cine.

_____

2. Tomás dio la invitación *a sus amigos.*

_____

3. El profesor habló *al estudiante* en español.

_____

Nombre _____ Fecha _____

Un poco más

A **Una ópera** Read the following advertisement that appeared in a Spanish newspaper.

B **Buscando informes** Answer the questions according to the information in the advertisement in Activity A.

1. ¿Qué temporada es?

_____

2. ¿Qué ópera presentan ahora?

_____

3. ¿Quién escribió la ópera?

_____

4. ¿Cuándo es el estreno (la primera función)?

_____

5. ¿En qué teatro es?

_____

6. ¿Dónde venden las entradas o localidades?

_____

C **Un tenor español** Read the following information that appeared in a short magazine clip.

LA LEGION DE HONOR PARA JOSE CARRERAS

CON LA CRUZ DE CABALLERO DE LA LEGION DE HONOR FRANCESA, OTORGADA POR EL PRESIDENTE JACQUES CHIRAC, FUE CONDECORADO EL TENOR ESPAÑOL JOSE CARRERAS, NO SOLO EN SU CALIDAD DE ARTISTA, SINO TAMBIEN POR SU LABOR COMO PRESIDENTE DE LA FUNDACION CONTRA LA LEUCEMIA, MAL DEL QUE EL CATALAN FUE VICTIMA HACE UNOS AÑOS, Y QUE LOGRO SUPERAR DESPUES DE UN TRASPLANTE DE MEDULA.

D **Información** Give the following information according to the clip in Activity C.

1. el nombre del tenor español _____

2. el nombre del presidente francés _____

3. enfermedad de la que sufrió el tenor _____

4. organización beneficiosa por la que trabaja Carreras _____

Un cantante famoso Read the following ad that appeared in a Puerto Rican newspaper.

 Preguntas In a word or two, answer the questions according to the ad in Activity E.

1. nombre del cantante

_____

2. fechas de su espectáculo

_____

3. orquesta que lo va a acompañar

_____

4. nombre del conductor de la orquesta

_____

5. dónde va a ser el concierto

_____

6. cuándo están a la venta los boletos

_____

Mi autobiografía

Everyone gets involved in different cultural activities. Write about a cultural activity that interests you and mention others that don't interest you. Do you watch a lot of television? What programs do you watch? Do you go to the movies often? When do you go? Do you enjoy the arts? If so, write about those that interest you.

Mi autobiografía

Capítulo 11
Un viaje en avión

Vocabulario   PALABRAS 1

A **Una tarjeta de embarque** Give the following information according to the boarding pass.

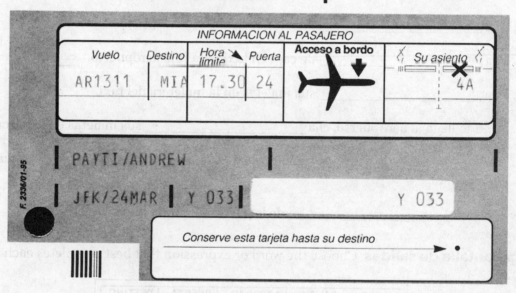

1. el nombre del pasajero _____

2. el nombre de la línea aérea _____

3. la hora de salida _____

4. la fecha del vuelo _____

5. el número del vuelo _____

6. el número de la puerta de salida _____

7. el número del asiento _____

8. el destino del vuelo _____

B **En el aeropuerto** Indicate whether each statement is true or false. Write **sí** or **no**.

1. _____ Cuando el pasajero llega al aeropuerto, tiene que facturar las maletas grandes.

2. _____ Es imposible abordar el avión con el equipaje de mano.

3. _____ Cuando el pasajero factura su equipaje, el agente pone un talón en cada maleta para identificar el destino.

4. _____ Cuando uno hace un viaje internacional, es decir un viaje a un país extranjero, es necesario llevar (tener) pasaporte.

5. _____ Antes de abordar el avión, los pasajeros tienen que pasar por el control de seguridad donde inspeccionan al pasajero y su equipaje de mano. Verifican si el pasajero lleva un arma de fuego—como una pistola, por ejemplo.

C **Un viaje en avión** Complete each sentence with the appropriate word(s).

1. Ella _____ un viaje en avión.

2. Ella _____ de casa en taxi para ir al aeropuerto.

3. Ella _____ sus maletas en la maletera del taxi.

4. Cuando llega al aeropuerto, ella _____ sus maletas en la báscula.

5. Ella _____ su equipaje. El agente _____ un talón en cada maleta.

6. Su avión _____ de la puerta de salida número siete.

D **La pantalla de salidas** Choose the word or expression that best completes each sentence.

VUELO	SALIDA	ABORDAR	PUERTA	DESTINO
UA 105	7:05	6:30	5	BUENOS AIRES
AA 731	7:30	7:00	12	LIMA
AV 701	8:15	7:45	2	BOGOTÁ

1. El vuelo 105 de la United sale a las _____.

   a. siete y cinco   **b.** seis y media   **c.** cinco

2. El vuelo que sale a las ocho y cuarto va a _____.

   a. Lima   **b.** Buenos Aires   **c.** Bogotá

3. Los pasajeros del vuelo 701 de Avianca pueden abordar el avión a las _____.

   a. ocho y cuarto   **b.** ocho menos cuarto   **c.** dos

4. El vuelo que sale de la puerta número doce va a _____.

   a. Buenos Aires   **b.** Lima   **c.** Bogotá

Vocabulario   PALABRAS 2

E   **¿Qué es o quién es?** Write the name of each place or person.

1. _____   2. _____   3. _____

4. _____   5. _____

F   **Palabras derivadas** Match each verb in the left-hand column with the corresponding noun in the right-hand column.

1. _____ asistir   **a.** el vuelo

2. _____ reclamar   **b.** el aterrizaje

3. _____ controlar   **c.** el despegue

4. _____ volar   **d.** el control

5. _____ inspeccionar   **e.** el/la asistente

6. _____ despegar   **f.** la inspección

7. _____ aterrizar   **g.** el reclamo

8. _____ llegar   **h.** la llegada

G **Diccionario** Give the word being defined.

1. el que trabaja a bordo del avión; sirve a los pasajeros

   _____

2. todo el personal a bordo de un avión

   _____

3. el comandante

   _____

4. los que viajan en el avión

   _____

5. el lugar donde inspeccionan o verifican los pasaportes

   _____

6. el lugar donde inspeccionan el equipaje de los pasajeros que llegan

   _____

Nombre _____ Fecha _____

Estructura

Hacer, poner, traer, salir en el presente

A **Un viaje** Make sentences using the expression **hacer un viaje.**

1. Yo / a España

_____

2. Yo / con mi primo

_____

3. Nosotros / en avión

_____

4. Mis hermanos no / a España

_____

5. Ellos / a México

_____

6. ¿Adónde / sus padres?

_____

7. Mis padres / a México también

_____

B **Haciendo la maleta** Complete each sentence with the correct form of **hacer, poner,** and **salir**.

1. Juan _____ la maleta. Él _____ una camisa en la

maleta. Él _____ para Málaga.

2. Nosotros _____ nuestra maleta. Nosotros _____

blue jeans en la maleta. Nosotros _____ la maleta porque

_____ para Cancún, México.

3. ¿Tú _____ tu maleta? ¿Para dónde _____?

4. Mis padres _____ su maleta. Ellos _____ muchas

cosas en la maleta. Ellos _____ su maleta porque

_____ para Miami.

5. Yo _____ mi maleta. Yo _____ blue jeans y T-shirts

en mi maleta. Yo _____ la maleta porque _____

para la Sierra de Guadarrama donde voy de camping.

C **Todos tenemos suerte.** These people are lucky because they are coming from a place they enjoyed a great deal. Complete each sentence with the correct form of **tener** and **venir.**

1. Yo _____ mucha suerte porque _____ de Toledo,
una ciudad fantástica cerca de Madrid.

2. Jesús y Juanita _____ mucha suerte porque _____

de Puerto Rico, una isla tropical en el mar Caribe que _____ playas
estupendas.

3. Nosotros _____ mucha suerte porque _____ de la
Ciudad de México, la fabulosa capital de nuestro país.

4. Jorge _____ mucha suerte porque _____ de Quito,
una ciudad colonial en los Andes.

5. Tú también _____ mucha suerte porque _____ de
Acapulco.

El presente progresivo

D **Un poco de gramática** Give the present participle of each of the following verbs.

1. volar _____

4. hacer _____

2. llegar _____

5. salir _____

3. comer _____

6. leer _____

E **¿Qué están haciendo?** Rewrite each sentence using the present progressive tense.

1. Los pasajeros embarcan.

_____

2. El asistente de vuelo mira (revisa) las tarjetas de embarque.

_____

3. Los pasajeros buscan su asiento.

_____

4. Ponen su equipaje de mano en el compartimiento sobre su asiento.

_____

5. La asistente de vuelo anuncia la salida.

_____

6. El avión despega.

_____

F **Un viaje** Complete each sentence with the present progressive of the verb(s) in parentheses.

1. Nosotros _____ un viaje. (hacer)

2. En este momento, nosotros_____ a una altura de 10.000

metros pero el avión todavía _____. (volar, subir)

3. Nosotros _____ los Andes. (sobrevolar)

4. Ahora el avión _____. (aterrizar)

5. Nosotros _____ al aeropuerto Jorge Chávez en Lima. (llegar)

G   **¿Qué hacen ahora?** Answer the questions according to the illustrations.

1. ¿Qué están haciendo Teresa y Cristóbal ahora?

_____

_____

2. ¿Qué está haciendo el señor Aparicio ahora?

_____

_____

3. ¿Qué estoy haciendo ahora?

_____

_____

4. ¿Qué estamos haciendo ahora?

_____

_____

Saber y conocer en el presente

H   **Lo que sé hacer** In complete sentences, write five things you know how to do.

1. _____

2. _____

3. _____

4. _____

5. _____

Nombre _____ Fecha _____

I **¿A quiénes conoces?** In complete sentences, write the names of five people you know.

1. _____

2. _____

3. _____

4. _____

5. _____

J **Un(a) buen(a) amigo(a)** Write a paragraph about a good friend. In the paragraph, answer the following questions: **¿Sabes su número de teléfono? ¿Cuál es? ¿Conoce él o ella a toda tu familia? ¿Conoces a toda su familia también? ¿Cuáles son algunas cosas que él o ella sabe hacer muy bien? ¿Sabes hacer las mismas cosas?**

_____

_____

_____

_____

_____

_____

_____

_____

K **Un viaje a Puerto Rico** Complete each sentence with the correct form of **saber** or **conocer.**

1. Miguel _____ que mañana va a salir para San Juan.

2. Él _____ el número de su vuelo y a qué hora va a salir.

3. Como Miguel es de Puerto Rico, él _____ a mucha gente en la isla.

4. Él _____ la historia de Puerto Rico también.

5. Él _____ que no tiene que llevar pasaporte a Puerto Rico.

6. Él _____ que Puerto Rico es un estado libre asociado de Estados Unidos.

Un poco màs

A **Un anuncio** Read the following ad that appeared in a San Juan newspaper.

B **La línea aérea** Answer the questions according to the information in the ad in Activity A.

1. ¿Cuál es el nombre de la línea aérea? _____

2. ¿De qué país es la compañía? _____

3. ¿Cuántos vuelos diarios tienen entre San Juan y la República Dominicana? _____

4. ¿Cuánto es la tarifa? _____

5. ¿A cuántos países vuela? _____

6. ¿Dónde está la oficina de Copa en Puerto Rico? _____

C **Para ir al aeropuerto** You are in Madrid and you plan to go to the airport. You want to take the airport bus. Fill in the following form at your hotel.

Aero CITY
Traslado aeropuerto

Hoja de Reservas

Rellene este cupón y confirme la hora de recogida en recepción.

Las recogidas se efectuarán en:
- **Hotel-Aeropuerto:** recepción del Hotel.
- **Aeropuerto-Hotel:** Parada Hotel Bus en la terminal correspondiente.

Todos los coches estan equipados con aire acondicionado y teléfono. El consumo telefónico se cobrará a razón de 14pts/paso. Los traslados podrán ser compartidos. Garantizamos un máx. de tres paradas.

Nombre		N° hab.
Fecha	N° pax	Terminal NACIONAL INTERNAC
N° vuelo		Hora vuelo

A rellenar por el personal del Hotel

Hotel	Recepcionista
Contacto AeroCity	Hora de recogida confirmada

Nombre		Aero CITY Traslado aeropuerto
Recepcionista	N° pax.	Importe
Fecha	Hora de recogida confirmada	

D **Un vuelo** Read the following advertisement.

E **Buscando informes** Answer the questions according to the information in the ad in Activity D.

1. ¿Cuándo pueden viajar los pasajeros? _____

2. ¿Cuándo tienen que comprar sus boletos o pasajes? _____

3. ¿Cómo son las tarifas? _____

4. ¿Son tarifas de ida y vuelta o de ida solamente? _____

F **Una tarjeta postal** Imagine you are in the airport and you are taking a trip. Tell your friend where you are going, what you have to do at the airport, and what time your flight is leaving.

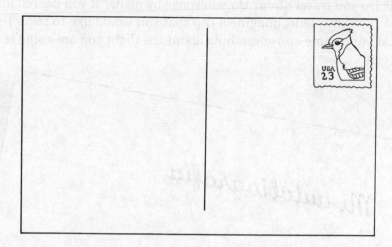

G **Las lenguas romances** Spanish shares a lot of vocabulary with the other Romance languages derived from Latin. Look at the expressions below in Spanish, French, Italian, and Portuguese. Notice how much you could understand at an airport in Paris, Rome, Lisbon, or Rio de Janeiro.

ESPAÑOL	FRANCÉS	ITALIANO	PORTUGUÉS
la línea aérea	la ligne aérienne	la linea aerea	a linha aérea
el vuelo	le vol	il vuolo	o vôo
el pasaporte	le passeport	il passaporto	o passaporte
la puerta	la porte	la porta	a porta
la tarjeta de embarque	la carte d'embarquement	la carta d'imbarco	a cartão de embarque
la aduana	la douane	la dogana	a alfândega
el destino	la destination	la destinazione	o destino
el billete (boleto)	le billet	il biglietto	o bilhete
el pasajero	le passager	il passaggero	o passageiro
el viaje	le voyage	il viaggio	a viagem

Read the following announcements in Spanish, French, and Italian. Do you think you would have any trouble understanding them if you were at an airport in Spain, France, or Italy?

ESPAÑOL

Iberia anuncia la salida de su vuelo ciento cinco con destino a Madrid. Embarque inmediato por la puerta número siete, por favor.

FRANCÉS

Air France annonce le départ de son vol cent cinq à destination de Paris. Embarquement immédiat par la porte numéro sept, s'il vous plaît.

ITALIANO

Alitalia anuncia la partenza del vuolo cento cinque a destinazione Roma. Imbarco immediato per la porta numero sette, per favore.

Mi autobiografía

Do you like to travel? Do you travel often? Do you travel by plane? If you do, tell about your experience(s). If you do not travel by plane, imagine a trip that you would like to take. Tell something about the airport near your home and something about the flight you are going to take. Include as many details as you can.

Mi autobiografía

CHECK-UP 3

A Match each statement with the appropriate illustration.

a   b   c

d   e

1. _____ La muchacha estornuda.   **4.** _____ Tiene fiebre y escalofríos.

2. _____ La muchacha está muy contenta.   **5.** _____ Guarda cama.

3. _____ Ella tiene dolor de cabeza.

B Complete each sentence with the appropriate word(s).

1. El médico ve a sus pacientes en su _____.

2. Tomás _____ la boca cuando el médico le _____ la garganta.

3. Gloria tiene fiebre y escalofríos y tiene dolor de estómago. El médico cree que tiene la

_____.

4. El farmacéutico despacha los _____ en la farmacia.

5. El enfermo tiene que tomar tres _____ cada día.

C Identify each item.

1. _____

2. _____

3. _____

4. _____

5. _____

D Answer the following questions.

1. ¿Qué tiempo hace en el verano?

_____

_____

2. ¿Qué tiempo hace en el invierno?

_____

_____

3. ¿Qué hace la gente en la playa?

_____

_____

4. ¿Qué hace la gente en una estación de esquí?

_____

_____

E Choose the correct answer for each question.

1. El joven vio una película.

   a. ¿Ah, sí? ¿Fue al cine?

   b. ¿Ah, sí? ¿Fue al teatro?

   c. ¿Ah, sí? ¿Fue al museo?

2. ¿Dónde hace cola?

   a. Delante de la pantalla.

   b. Delante del telón.

   c. Delante de la taquilla.

3. ¿Qué compras para ir al teatro o al cine?

   a. Butacas.

   b. Entradas.

   c. Obras.

4. ¿Está doblada la película?

   a. Sí, hay dos.

   b. No, lleva subtítulos.

   c. Sí, en la pantalla.

5. ¿Por qué aplaudieron?

   a. Les gustó el espectáculo.

   b. Dieron una representación de **Bodas de Sangre.**

   c. El autor escribió una obra buena.

F Complete each sentence with the appropriate word(s).

1. Vamos al _____ si vamos a tomar un vuelo.

2. Tenemos tres maletas. Las quiero _____ para Madrid.

3. El _____ para Madrid sale a las seis cuarenta de la

_____ número ocho.

4. Antes de abordar el avión, los pasajeros tienen que pasar por _____

_____.

5. El _____ y los _____ de vuelo son miembros de
la tripulación.

G Complete each sentence with the correct form of **ser** or **estar**.

1. Ella no _____ triste. _____ contenta.

2. Isabel _____ una alumna muy buena. Ella _____ muy seria.

3. Isabel _____ de Puerto Rico y yo _____ de México.

4. Y ahora Isabel _____ en México y yo _____ en Puerto Rico.

5. Yo _____ en San Juan.

6. San Juan _____ en el nordeste de Puerto Rico.

7. La capital _____ muy bonita.

H Complete each sentence with the correct form of the preterite of the verb(s) in parentheses.

1. Ellos _____ al cine. (ir)

2. Yo _____ las entradas en la taquilla. (comprar)

3. Nosotros _____ una película muy buena. (ver)

4. ¿ _____ tú a Carlos en el cine? Él también _____. (Ver, ir)

5. Sí, él me _____ y me _____. (ver, hablar)

6. ¿A qué hora _____ ustedes del cine? (salir)

7. Luego (nosotros) _____ a comer algo. (ir)

8. Carlos _____ una pizza. (comer)

9. Pero yo no _____ nada. _____ un refresco. (comer, Tomar)

10. ¿Qué _____ tú? (tomar)

I Complete the conversation with the correct pronouns.

—Enrique, ¿ _____ vio Carolina?
            1

—Sí, ella _____ vio delante de la escuela después de las clases. Pero yo no _____ vi.
          2   3

—¿No _____ viste?
          4

—No. Luego ella _____ habló.
              5

—¿Y tú _____ hablaste a ella también?
          6

—Sí, _____ hablé. Y _____ invité a tu fiesta.
         7   8

—¡Ah! ¡Qué bien! Ahora no _____ tengo que escribir una invitación.
                                          9

J Answer the following questions.

1. ¿Haces un viaje?

_____

2. ¿Vas a México?

_____

3. ¿Haces un viaje en avión?

_____

4. ¿A qué hora sales?

_____

5. ¿Sabes a qué hora vas a llegar a México?

_____

6. ¿Conoces a México?

_____

Nombre _____ Fecha _____

K Complete with the correct form of **saber** or **conocer**.

1. ¿ _____ tú a Alejandra Pérez?

2. Sí, yo la _____ bien.

3. ¿ _____ (tú) su número de teléfono?

4. No, yo no _____ su número.

5. Pero Carlos _____ donde vive.

6. ¿Ah, sí? ¿Carlos la _____ también?

L Rewrite each sentence, using the progressive tense as in the model.

Esquían.
Están esquiando.

1. Esquían en el agua.

_____

2. Tomo el sol.

_____

3. ¿Ustedes comen en la playa?

_____

4. Escriben tarjetas postales.

_____

Capítulo 12

Una gira

Vocabulario   PALABRAS 1

 ¿Qué es? Identify each item.

1. _____

2. _____

3. _____

4. _____

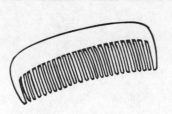

5. _____

6. _____

B **El cuerpo** Identify as many parts of the body as you can in Spanish.

1. _____   8. _____

2. _____   9. _____

3. _____   10. _____

4. _____   11. _____

5. _____   12. _____

6. _____   13. _____

7. _____

C **Frases originales** Make up sentences using a word or expression from each column.

| El joven La joven | levantarse lavarse mirarse ponerse sentarse cepillarse | una falda azul a las siete de la mañana los dientes en el espejo la cara tarde a la mesa |

1. _____

2. _____

3. _____

4. _____

5. _____

6. _____

Vocabulario   PALABRAS 2

D **¿Qué es?** Answer the question according to the illustrations.

¿Qué pone la joven en la mochila?

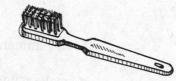

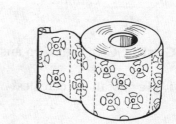

1. _____ 2. _____ 3. _____

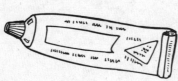

4. _____ 5. _____ 6. _____

E **Una gira** Complete each sentence with the appropriate word(s).

1. Los amigos están viajando por un país europeo. Los amigos están viajando por

_____.

2. Están haciendo un viaje que no cuesta mucho. Están haciendo un viaje _____.

3. Lo están pasando muy bien. Se _____ mucho.

4. Ellos no andan a pie. Van en _____.

5. No duermen en una cama. Duermen en su _____.

6. No pasan la noche en un hotel lujoso. Pasan la noche en _____

_____.

F **Palabras relacionadas** Match each word in the left-hand column with a related word in the right-hand column.

1. _____ cepillar   **a.** dentífrico

2. _____ desayunar   **b.** la comida

3. _____ los dientes   **c.** la diversión

4. _____ peinar   **d.** el cepillo

5. _____ sentarse   **e.** el peine

6. _____ comer   **f.** la caminata

7. _____ enrollar   **g.** el desayuno

8. _____ divertirse   **h.** el viaje

9. _____ viajar   **i.** el asiento

10. _____ caminar   **j.** el rollo

G **Gustos** Give your own answers.

1. ¿Te gustan los cereales?

_____

2. ¿Te gustan las naranjas?

_____

3. ¿Te gusta el jugo de naranja?

_____

4. Para el desayuno, ¿te gustan más los huevos o los cereales?

_____

5. ¿Te gusta comer en la cafetería de la escuela?

_____

Estructura

Verbos reflexivos

A **Preguntas personales** Answer the following questions.

1. ¿Cómo te llamas?

_____

2. ¿A qué hora te levantas?

_____

3. ¿Dónde te desayunas?

_____

4. ¿Te cepillas los dientes después del desayuno?

_____

5. Por la mañana, ¿te bañas o tomas una ducha?

_____

6. ¿Te miras en el espejo cuando te peinas?

_____

B **Un día típico** Complete each sentence with the correct reflexive pronoun(s).

1. Yo _____ despierto y _____ levanto enseguida.

2. Mi hermano y yo _____ levantamos a la misma hora.

3. Yo _____ lavo y luego él _____ lava.

4. Nosotros no _____ lavamos al mismo tiempo en el cuarto de baño.

5. Mis amigos _____ cepillan los dientes después de cada comida.

6. Y ellos _____ lavan las manos antes de comer.

C **Yo** Complete the paragraph with the appropriate words.

Yo _____ lavo _____ manos y _____ cara. _____ cepillo _____ dientes y _____ cepillo
    1   2   3   4   5   6

_____ pelo. Yo _____ pongo _____ ropa.
  7   8   9

Verbos reflexivos de cambio radical

D **La rutina** Complete each sentence with the correct present-tense form of the verb(s).

1. Yo _____ y me levanto enseguida. (despertarse)

2. Mi hermana y yo bajamos a la cocina y _____ a la mesa.
   (sentarse)

3. Después de las clases, yo _____ con mis amigos.

   Nosotros _____ mucho. (divertirse, divertirse)

4. Cuando yo _____, _____
   enseguida. (acostarse, dormirse)

5. Y tú, ¿ _____ enseguida cuando

   _____? (dormirse, acostarse)

E **En el pasado** Rewrite each sentence in the preterite.

1. Ellos se sientan a la mesa.

   _____

2. Él se acuesta a la medianoche.

   _____

3. Desgraciadamente yo no me duermo enseguida.

   _____

4. Los amigos se divierten mucho.

   _____

5. ¿A qué hora te acuestas?

   _____

6. Yo me despierto tarde.

   _____

7. Nosotros nos sentamos a la mesa para tomar el desayuno.

   _____

F **¿Pronombre o no?** Complete with a pronoun when necessary.

1. Yo _____ llamo Paco. Y tú, ¿cómo _____ llamas?

2. Yo _____ llamo a mi amigo Alejandro.

3. Ellos _____ acuestan temprano.

4. Ellos _____ acuestan temprano al bebé.

5. _____ lavo la cara varias veces al día.

6. Una vez a la semana _____ lavo a mi perro.

7. Ella es muy graciosa. Siempre _____ divierte a sus amigos.

8. Todos _____ divierten cuando están con ella.

9. ¿Qué _____ pones en la mochila?

10. Hace frío. _____ pongo el anorak.

Nombre _____ Fecha _____

Un poco màs

A **Unos anuncios** Read the following ads for health and cosmetic products.

Champú TIMOTEI,
frasco de 500 mL
+ acondicionador
de 300 mL gratis,
2,70 €
El litro sale a 5,40 €

Papel higiénico
2 CAPAS
Papel higiénico
2 FOLHAS

①
Papel higiénico
12 rollos
1,35 €

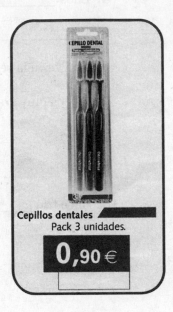

Cepillos dentales
Pack 3 unidades.
0,90 €

B **Sinónimos** Find another term for each of the following in the ads in Activity A.

1. cepillos de dientes _____

2. botella de 500 mL _____

C **Preguntas** Answer the questions according to the information in the ads in Activity A.

1. ¿Cuánto cuestan los cepillos de dientes? _____

2. ¿Cuál es el precio de un litro del champú ? _____

3. ¿En paquetes de cuántos rollos viene el papel higiénico? _____

4. ¿Cuántos cepillos dentales hay en un pak? _____

5. ¿Cuánto cuesta 12 rollos de papel higiénico? _____

6. ¿Qué es gratis si compras el champú? _____

D   **Afeitadora** Read the following advertisement.

Afeitadora   6680   CLS
- Sistema triple afeitado
- Cabezal basculante
- Dispensador automático del acondicionador
- Recargable: 50 minutos de autonomía
- Indicador de baja carga.

142 €

E   **La tienda** Answer according to the information in the ad in Activity D.

1. ¿Qué es la palabra en inglés por **afeitadora?** _____

2. ¿Cómo se llama la afeitadora? _____

3. ¿Qué dispensa la afeitadora? _____

4. ¿Cuánto cuesta la afeitadora? _____

5. ¿Por cuánto tiempo puede usar la afeitadora sin recargarlo? _____

Mi autobiografía

Every day there are routine activities we all have to do. Give as much information as you can about your daily routine. Tell what you usually do each day. Tell what time you usually do it. Is your weekend **(el fin de semana)** routine the same as your weekday **(durante la semana, días laborables)** routine or not?

Capítulo 13
Un viaje en tren

Vocabulario   PALABRAS 1

A **¿Qué es o quién es?** Identify each item or person.

1. _____

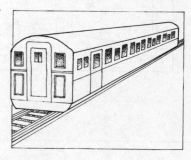

2. _____

3. _____

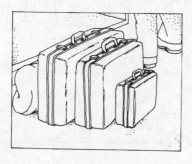

4. _____

5. _____

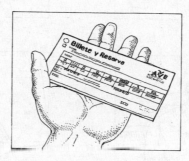

6. _____

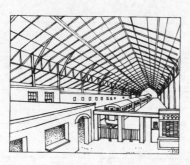

7. _____

8. _____

9. _____

B **En el andén** Write a paragraph describing the illustrations.

_____

_____

_____

_____

_____

_____

_____

_____

_____

Vocabulario   PALABRAS 2

C **Lo contrario** Match the word or expression in the left-hand column with its opposite in the right-hand column.

1. _____ subir al tren

2. _____ libre

3. _____ a tiempo

4. _____ el billete de ida y vuelta

5. _____ la salida

a. tarde

b. bajar del tren

c. el billete sencillo

d. la llegada

e. ocupado

D **El sinónimo** Match the word or expression in the left-hand column with a word or expression that means the same in the right-hand column.

1. _____ el mozo

2. _____ la ventanilla

3. _____ el vagón

4. _____ el billete

5. _____ transbordar

6. _____ con retraso

a. la boletería

b. cambiar de tren

c. con una demora

d. el maletero

e. el boleto

f. el coche

E **Frases originales** Make up a sentence according to each illustration.

1. _____
   _____

2. _____
   _____

3. _____
   _____

4. _____
   _____

5. _____
   _____

Estructura

Hacer, querer y venir en el pretérito

A **En el pasado** Rewrite each sentence in the preterite.

1. No lo quiero hacer.

   _____

2. No lo hago.

   _____

3. No vengo.

   _____

4. ¿Por qué no lo quieres hacer?

   _____

5. ¿Ustedes no lo hacen?

   _____

6. ¿Por qué no vienen?

   _____

7. Nosotros lo hacemos a tiempo.

   _____

Verbos irregulares en el pretérito

B **Un accidente, pero no serio** Complete each sentence with the correct preterite form of the verb(s) in parentheses.

1. Unos cien pasajeros _____ a bordo del tren cuando

   _____ lugar (ocurrió) el accidente. (estar, tener)

2. Nosotros no _____ nada del accidente. (saber)

3. Como ustedes no _____ nada, no _____ hacer nada, ¿verdad? (saber, poder)

4. Exactamente. Pero cuando ellos no llegaron a mi casa, yo _____ una llamada telefónica. (hacer)

5. Pero yo _____ que esperar mucho tiempo para saber algo porque nadie contestó el (al) teléfono. (tener)

C **Un viaje por España** Complete each sentence with the correct preterite form of the verb(s) in parentheses.

1. Ellos _____ un viaje a España. (hacer)

2. Ellos _____ por todo el país. (andar)

3. Desgraciadamente no _____ ir a Galicia en el noroeste porque no

   _____ bastante tiempo. (poder, tener)

4. Ellos _____ casi un mes entero en Andalucía, en el sur. (estar)

Nombre _____ Fecha _____

D **El tren** Rewrite each sentence in the preterite.

1. Yo hago un viaje con mi hermana.

_____

2. Hacemos el viaje en tren.

_____

3. No queremos hacer el viaje en coche.

_____

4. El tren está completo.

_____

5. Nosotros no podemos encontrar un asiento libre.

_____

6. Nosotros estamos de pie en el pasillo.

_____

7. Nosotros tenemos que transbordar en Segovia.

_____

8. Podemos encontrar un asiento libre en el otro tren.

_____

9. Estamos muy cómodos en este tren.

_____

E **En el pasado** Rewrite the sentences in the past.

1. No lo hago porque no lo quiero hacer.

_____

2. Y él no lo hace porque no lo puede hacer.

_____

3. Ellos no vienen porque no tienen el carro.

_____

4. Él no sabe nada porque nadie le quiere hablar.

_____

5. No puedes porque no quieres.

_____

6. No estamos porque tenemos que hacer otra cosa.

_____

F **¿Qué dices?** Complete each sentence with the correct form of the present tense of the verb **decir**.

1. Yo _____ que vamos a ir a Sevilla.

2. Y él _____ que vamos a tomar el AVE—el tren rápido.

3. Todos ellos nos _____ que Sevilla es una maravilla.

4. Nosotros les _____ que nos va a ser un placer tener la oportunidad de visitar a Sevilla.

5. Teresa _____ que quiere estudiar en Sevilla.

6. Yo le _____ que hay muchas escuelas buenas en Sevilla para aprender el español.

Un poco más

A **Un horario** Look at the following schedule for trains between Madrid and Málaga.

B **Información** Answer the questions according to the train schedule in Activity A.

1. ¿De qué estación en Madrid salen los trenes? _____

2. ¿A qué hora sale el primer tren de la mañana para Málaga? _____

3. ¿Y a qué hora sale el primer tren de Málaga para Madrid? _____

4. ¿A qué hora llega el primer tren a Málaga? _____

5. ¿Cuántas paradas hace el tren número 9136 entre Madrid y Málaga? _____

6. Hay un tren que no hace ninguna parada entre Málaga y Madrid. ¿A qué hora sale de

Málaga el tren? _____

C **El billete** Look at the train ticket.

71	Nº D 239863	Indicaciones especiales	BILLETE + RESERVA	EL	0094 U5PA2010
	LARGO RECORRIDO RENFE			Sello de emisión	00000000 2660
	C.I.F. G-28016749				20:41
	201012226593 40117				

DE ────────→ A	CLASE	30 FECHA	🕐 HORA SALIDA	TIPO DE TREN	COCHE	Nº PLAZA	DEPARTAMENTO	Nº TREN
CHAMARTIN A CORUNA	C	23.05	21.45	ESTRELL	0041	045A	DOBLE	00851
HORA DE LLEGADA-->:			08.45			CLIMATIZ.	FAMILIA	

Tarifa   010 TARIFA GENERAL -TG- 044
Forma de pago   METALICO   Euros   ***107.00

Incluido S.O.V. e I.V.A.

(left margin:) PROHIBIDO FUMAR FUERA DE LA ZONA RESERVADA   CONSERVESE HASTA EL FINAL DEL VIAJE

D **El tren** Answer the questions according to the information on the train ticket in Activity C.

1. ¿Es un billete para un tren de largo recorrido o para un tren de cercanías?

_____

2. ¿De qué estación en Madrid sale el tren? _____

3. ¿A qué hora sale de Madrid? _____

4. ¿A qué hora llega a La Coruña? _____

5. ¿Para qué día es el billete? _____

6. ¿Cuánto costó el billete? _____

E **Preguntas** Answer according to the information on the ticket in Activity C.

1. Something on the ticket indicates that the train is air-conditioned. What is it?

_____

2. The ticket indicates that the form of payment was _____.

What does **metálico** refer to? _____

Nombre _____ Fecha _____

F **Transportes** Read the following information about transportation in Madrid.

G **¿Sí o no?** Indicate whether the following statements are true or false according to the information in Activity F. Write **sí** or **no.**

1. _____ Hay tres grandes estaciones de ferrocarril en Madrid.

2. _____ El AVE sale de la estación de Atocha.

3. _____ En Madrid hay numerosas líneas de autobuses urbanos.

4. _____ El metro va a muy pocas regiones de la ciudad.

5. _____ El precio del billete del autobús es el mismo que el precio del billete del metro.

6. _____ El aeropuerto internacional de Madrid se llama Barajas.

7. _____ El aeropuerto de Barajas está al norte de la ciudad de Madrid.

Mi autobiografía

Do you ever travel by train? If so, tell about one of your train trips. If you have never taken a train trip, imagine you are traveling by train through Spain. Write about your trip. Make up as much information as you can.

Mi autobiografía

WORKBOOK

Capítulo 14
En el restaurante

Vocabulario   PALABRAS 1

A **¿Qué es o quién es?** Identify each item or person.

1. _____

2. _____

3. _____

4. _____

5. _____

B   **¿Qué es?** Identify each item.

   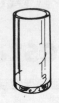   

1. _____   2. _____   3. _____

4. _____   5. _____

6. _____   7. _____

C   **Vamos a comer.** Answer the following questions.

1. ¿Qué quieres hacer cuando tienes hambre?

_____

2. Y cuando tienes sed, ¿qué quieres hacer?

_____

3. Cuando vas a un restaurante, ¿qué le pides al mesero?

_____

4. ¿Quién trabaja en la cocina para preparar las comidas?

_____

5. ¿Quién sirve la comida?

_____

Vocabulario   PALABRAS 2

D **Comestibles** Answer the following questions.

1. ¿Cuáles son cuatro carnes?

_____

_____

2. ¿Cuáles son tres mariscos?

_____

_____

3. ¿Cuáles son seis vegetales?

_____

_____

E **Una reservación** Complete the following conversation.

—¡Diga!

—Quisiera _____ una mesa, por favor.
                       1

—Sí, señor. ¿Para _____?
                            2

—Para mañana a las veinte treinta.

—¿Y para _____ personas?
                   3

—Para seis.

—¿A _____ de quién, por _____?
            4   5

—A _____ de González.
           6

—Conforme, señor. Una mesa para seis _____ para
                                                          7

_____ a las veinte treinta a _____ de González.
        8   9

F **La carne** Answer the following questions.

1. ¿Comes hamburguesas? ¿Qué te gusta comer con la hamburguesa?

_____

_____

_____

2. ¿Comes cerdo? ¿Qué te gusta comer con el cerdo?

_____

_____

_____

3. ¿Comes biftec? ¿Qué te gusta comer con el biftec?

_____

_____

_____

4. ¿Comes cordero? ¿Qué te gusta comer con el cordero?

_____

_____

_____

Estructura

Verbos con el cambio e → i en el presente

A **El presente** Rewrite the sentences, changing **nosotros** to **yo** in the present tense.

1. Nosotros pedimos un cóctel de camarones.

   _____

2. Freímos el pescado.

   _____

3. Servimos la ensalada antes del plato principal.

   _____

4. Seguimos una dieta sana.

   _____

B **En el restaurante** Complete each sentence with the correct present-tense form of the verb(s) in parentheses.

1. El mesero les _____ a los clientes lo que ellos le _____.
   (servir, pedir)

2. Si el cliente _____ papas fritas, el cocinero las _____.
   (pedir, freír)

3. A veces si hay un plato que me gusta mucho, yo lo _____ otra vez. (pedir)

4. Si el mesero me _____ bien, yo le dejo una propina. (servir)

C **¿Qué le gusta?** Answer the questions according to the model.

   ¿Le gusta a Juanita el pollo?
   Sí, y siempre lo pide.

1. ¿Te gustan los huevos fritos?

   _____

2. ¿Les gusta a ustedes la ensalada con aceite y vinagre?

   _____

3. ¿Les gusta a Carlos y a Felipe el biftec?

   _____

Verbos con el cambio e → i, o → u en el pretérito

D **En el restaurante** Answer each question according to the cue.

1. ¿Qué pediste? (arroz con pollo)

_____

2. ¿Te gustó el plato? (sí, mucho)

_____

3. ¿Repetiste el plato cuando fuiste al restaurante la segunda vez? (no)

_____

4. ¿Qué pediste la segunda vez? (el cerdo asado)

_____

5. ¿Qué plato preferiste? (no sé)

_____

6. ¿Te gustaron los dos platos? (sí)

_____

7. Después de comer mucho, ¿dormiste bien? (no, no muy bien)

_____

E **Marcos** Complete the following paragraph according to the information in Activity D.

Marcos _____ un arroz con pollo. Le _____ mucho.
                1   **2**

Pero cuando volvió al restaurante no _____ el mismo plato.
                                         3

_____ el cerdo asado. No sabe qué plato _____
      4   **5**

porque le _____ los dos platos. Pero despúes de comer tanto, él no
             6

_____ muy bien.
     7

Un poco màs

A **Un restaurante** Read this ad for a restaurant on the outskirts of Madrid.

RESTAURANTE
Los Remos
(antes Parque Moroso)
PRIMERA CASA EN PESCADOS Y MARISCOS
AMBIENTE SELECTO • VIVEROS PROPIOS
Ctra. Coruña, km. 12,700
Telfs. 91 307 72 30 - 91 307 73 36
ABIERTO DOMINGOS MEDIODIA
P PARKING PROPIO

B **Buscando informes** Answer the questions based on the information in the ad in Activity A. Write the answers in Spanish.

1. What's the name of the restaurant?

_____

2. What do they serve in this restaurant?

_____

3. What's its former name?

_____

4. When is the restaurant open on Sundays?

_____

El menú Look at the menu for the Casa Botín, a restaurant considered to be the oldest in the world.

C A R T A

I.V.A. 7% INCLUIDO

ENTRADAS

Jugos de tomate, naranja	4,10
Pimientos asados con bacalao	9,80
Lomo ibérico de bellota	23,05
Jamón ibérico de bellota	25,25
Surtido ibérico de bellota	21,60
Melón con jamón	21,40
Queso (manchego)	8,95
Ensalada riojana	9,50
Ensalada de lechuga y tomate	4,90
ENSALADA BOTÍN (con pollo y jamón)	12,20
Ensalada de rape y langostinos	26,30
Ensalada de endivias con perdiz	21,20
Morcilla de Burgos	7,50
Croquetas de pollo y jamón	8,95
Manitas de cochinillo rebozadas	8,05
Salmón ahumado	20,30

SOPAS

Sopa al cuarto de hora (de pescados).................	16,25
SOPA DE AJO CON HUEVO.............................	5,95
Caldo de ave	4,90
Gazpacho	8,20

HUEVOS

Revuelto de la casa (morcilla y patatas)	8,50
Huevos revueltos con espárragos trigueros	10,15
Huevos revueltos con salmón ahumado	10,75
Tortilla de gambas	10,75

VERDURAS

Espárragos con mahonesa	13,65
Menestra de verduras salteadas con jamón ibérico....	12,00
Alcachofas salteadas con jamón ibérico	9,05
Judías verdes con jamón ibérico	9,05
Setas a la segoviana	9,85
Patatas fritas	3,75
Patatas asadas	3,75

PESCADOS

Angulas .... (según mercado)......................	
ALMEJAS BOTIN	24,05
Langostinos con mahonesa	38,05
Gambas al ajillo	27,50
Gambas a la plancha	27,50
Cazuela de pescados	28,85
Rape en salsa..	26,65
Merluza al horno o frita	31,50
Lenguado frito, al horno o a la plancha (pieza)	25,55
Calamares fritos	15,80
CHIPIRONES EN SU TINTA (arroz blanco)	16,75

ASADOS Y PARRILLAS

COCHINILLO ASADO......................................	23,60
CORDERO ASADO..	25,50
Pollo asado 1/2	9,70
Pollo en cacerola 1/2	12,85
Perdiz estofada (pieza)	25,10
Filete de ternera a la plancha	18,90
Escalope de ternera	19,20
Ternera asada con guisantes	19,20
Solomillo a la plancha	27,50
SOLOMILLO BOTIN (al champiñón)	27,50
"Entrecotte" de cebón a la plancha.....................	25,80

POSTRES

Cuajada..	6,60
Tarta helada..	6,65
Tarta de la casa (crema y bizcocho)....................	6,75
Tarta de chocolate..	7,30
Tarta de frambuesa	8,25
Pastel ruso (crema de praliné)...........................	8,00
Flan de la casa	4,25
Flan de la casa con nata	6,90
Helado de chocolate o caramelo	5,20
Helado de vainilla con salsa de chocolate	5,30
Surtido de buñuelos..	8,75
Hojaldre de crema	7,40
Piña natural al dry-sack	6,20
Fresón con nata...	7,80
Sorbete de limón..	5,95
Melón	6,55
Bartolillos (sábados y domingos)	7,30

MENU DE LA CASA

(Primavera - Verano)

Precio: 41,65 euros

Gazpacho
Cochinillo asado
Helado
Pan, vino, cerveza o agua mineral

CAFE 2,20 - PAN 1,05 - MANTEQUILLA 1,30

HORAS DE SERVICIO: ALMUERZO, de 1:00 A 4:00 - CENA, de 8:00 A 12:00

ABIERTO TODOS LOS DIAS   HAY HOJAS DE RECLAMACION

Nombre _____ Fecha _____

D **¿Cómo se dice... ?** Find the Spanish equivalent of each of the following dishes.

1. chicken and ham croquettes _____

2. melon with ham _____

3. smoked salmon _____

4. garlic soup with egg _____

5. asparagus with mayonnaise _____

6. seafood casserole _____

7. clams Botín _____

8. sauteed artichokes with Iberian ham _____

9. 1/2 roasted chicken _____

10. grilled veal filet _____

E **En el restaurante** Answer the questions according to the information on the menu in Activity C.

1. ¿Es necesario pagar el pan y la mantequilla? _____

2. ¿ Cuánto es el pan? _____ ¿Y la mantequilla? _____

3. ¿Qué comidas sirven en el restaurante? _____

4. ¿A qué hora sirven el almuerzo? _____

5. ¿A qué hora sirven la cena? _____

6. ¿Cuándo está abierto el restaurante? _____

Mi autobiografía

Tell whether or not you like to eat in a restaurant. If you do, tell which restaurant(s) you go to. Give a description of a typical dinner out. You know quite a few words for foods in Spanish. Write about those foods you like and those foods you do not like.

Mi autobiografía

CHECK-UP 4

A Identify each item.

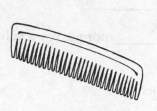

1. _____

2. _____

3. _____

4. _____

5. _____

6. _____

B Complete each sentence with the appropriate word(s).

1. Ella _____ los dientes con el cepillo de dientes.

2. Él _____ con una navaja.

3. Ella _____ la ropa en el cuarto de dormir.

4. Ellos toman el _____ en la cocina.

5. Ella _____ a las once de la noche.

WORKBOOK
Copyright © by The McGraw-Hill Companies, Inc.

¡Buen viaje! Level 1 Check-Up 4 ∞ **181**

C   Choose an expression from the list below to complete each sentence.

> la sala de espera   el quiosco
> la ventanilla   andén
> un billete sencillo   el tablero de llegadas y salidas
> un billete de ida y vuelta el mozo

1. Los pasajeros sacan (compran) sus billetes en _____.

2. Voy a comprar _____ porque voy a volver
aquí.

3. _____ ayuda a los pasajeros con sus maletas.

4. Compran periódicos y revistas en _____.

5. El tren para Córdoba va a salir del _____ tres.

D   Identify each item.

1. _____

2. _____

3. _____

4. _____

5. _____

WORKBOOK

6. _____   7. _____   8. _____

9. _____   10. _____

E Complete each sentence with the correct verb from the following list.

levantarse	**lavarse**	**despertarse**	**ponerse**
cepillarse	**peinarse**	**acostarse**	**desayunarse**
mirarse	**divertirse**		

1. El joven _____ a las seis y media de la mañana.

2. Antes de tomar el desayuno yo _____ las manos y la cara.

3. Después de comer, nosotros _____ los dientes.

4. Ellos _____ en el espejo cuando

_____ .

5. ¿Por qué no _____ (tú) la chaqueta? Está haciendo un poco frío.

6. ¿A qué hora _____ ustedes por la noche?

7. Yo _____ mucho cuando estoy con ellos. Son muy graciosos.

F Rewrite each sentence in the preterite.

1. Nosotros hacemos un viaje.

_____

2. Yo hago el viaje en tren y ellos lo hacen en avión.

_____

3. No podemos ir juntos.

_____

4. Ellos no quieren salir el sábado.

_____

5. Por eso, ellos tienen que tomar el avión.

_____

G Complete with the correct present-tense form of the verb **decir**.

Yo _____ que sí y ellos _____ que sí. Todos (nosotros)
　　　　　1　　　　　　　　　　　　　　　　　2

_____ que sí. Así, estamos de acuerdo.
　　　3

H Complete each sentence with the correct form of the verb(s) in parentheses.

1. Cuando yo voy a un restaurante, siempre _____ un biftec. (pedir)

2. Yo lo _____ a término medio. ¿Cómo lo _____ (tú)?
(pedir, pedir)

3. Los meseros _____ a los clientes en el restaurante. (servir)

4. Cuando nosotros _____ papas fritas, el cocinero las _____.
(pedir, freír)

I Complete the following paragraph with the correct preterite-tense forms of the verb **pedir**.

Yo _____ un biftec y él _____ pollo. Los dos (nosotros)
　　　　　1　　　　　　　　　　　　　　　　　2

_____ papas fritas. ¿Qué _____ tú? Y ¿qué
　　　3　　　　　　　　　　　　　　　　4

_____ tu amigo(a)?
　　　5

Audio Activities

CANCIONES

Las mañanitas

Éstas son las mañanitas,
Que cantaba el rey David,
Pero no eran tan bonitas,
Como las cantan aquí.

Despierta, mi bien, despierta,
Mira que ya amaneció.
Ya los pajarillos cantan,
La luna ya se metió.

Cielito lindo

Ese lunar que tienes, cielito lindo,
Junto a la boca,
No se lo des a nadie, cielito lindo,
Que a mí me toca.

Ay, ay, ay, ay,
Canta y no llores,
Porque cantando,
Se alegran cielito lindo,
Los corazones.

De colores

De colores, de colores
Se visten los campos en la primavera,
De colores, de colores
Son los pajarillos que vienen de fuera,
De colores, de colores es el arco iris
Que vemos lucir,
Y por eso los grandes amores
De muchos colores me gustan a mí,
Y por eso los grandes amores
De muchos colores me gustan a mí.

Guantanamera

Yo soy un hombre sincero,
De donde crece la palma.
Yo soy un hombre sincero,
De donde crece la palma,
Y antes de morirme quiero,
Echar mis versos del alma.

Guantanamera, guajira, Guantanamera,
Guantanamera, guajira, Guantanamera.

Mi verso es de un verde claro,
Y de un carmín encendido,
Mi verso es de un verde claro,
Y de un carmín encendido,
Mi verso es un ciervo herido,
Que busca en el monte amparo.

Guantanamera, guajira, Guantanamera,
Guantanamera, guajira, Guantanamera.

Eres tú

Como una promesa eres tú, eres tú,
Como una mañana de verano,
Como una sonrisa eres tú, eres tú.
Así, así, eres tú.

Toda mi esperanza eres tú, eres tú,
Como una lluvia fresca de mis manos,
Como fuerte brisa eres tú, eres tú,
Así, así, eres tú.

Eres tú como el agua de mi fuente,
Eres tú el fuego de mi hogar.

Como mi poema eres tú, eres tú,
Como una guitarra en la noche,
Como mi horizonte eres tú, eres tú,
Así, así, eres tú.

Como una promesa eres tú, eres tú,
etc.

San Fermín

Uno de enero, dos de febrero,
Tres de marzo, cuatro de abril,
Cinco de mayo, seis de junio,
Siete de julio, ¡San Fermín!

Me he de comer esa tuna

Guadalajara en un llano
México en una laguna,
Guadalajara en un llano
México en una laguna.
Me he de comer esa tuna,
Me he de comer esa tuna,
Me he de comer esa tuna,
Aunque me espine la mano.

Dicen que soy hombre malo
Malo y mal averiguado.
Dicen que soy hombre malo
Malo y mal averiguado.
Porque me comí un durazno,
Porque me comí un durazno,
Porque me comí un durazno,
De corazón colorado.

El águila siendo animal
Se retrató en el dinero.
El águila siendo animal
Se retrató en el dinero.
Para subir al nopal,
Para subir al nopal,
Para subir al nopal,
Pidió permiso primero.

Quizás, quizás, quizás

Siempre que te pregunto,
Que cuándo, cómo y dónde,
Tú siempre me respondes,
  quizás, quizás, quizás…
Y así pasan los días,
Yo yo desesperando,
Y tú, tú contestando,
  quizás, quizás, quizás…
Estás perdiendo el tiempo,
Pensando, pensando,
Por lo que tú más quieras
Hasta cuándo,
Hasta cuándo…
Y así pasan los días,
Y yo desesperando,
Y tú, tú contestando,
  quizás, quizás, quizás.

La última noche

La última noche que pasé contigo,
La llevo guardada como fiel testigo,
De aquellos momentos en que fuiste mía
Y hoy quiero borrarla de mi ser…
La última noche que pasé contigo
Quisiera olvidarla pero no he podido,
La última noche que pasé contigo,
Tengo que olvidarla de mi ayer…
  ¿Por qué te fuiste,
  Aquella noche,
  Por qué te fuiste,
  Sin regresar?
  Y me dejaste,
  Aquella noche,
  Como recuerdo
  De tu traición…
La última noche que pasé contigo,
La llevo guardada como fiel testigo,
De aquellos momentos en que fuiste mía.
Y hoy quiero borrarla de mi ser.
Y hoy quiero borrarla de mi ser.

El reloj

Reloj, no marques las horas,
Porque voy a enloquecer,
Ella se irá para siempre,
Cuando amanezca otra vez.
No más nos queda esta noche,
Para vivir nuestro amor,
Y su tic-toc me recuerda
Mi irremediable dolor.
Reloj, detén tu camino,
Porque mi vida se apaga,
Ella es la estrella que alumbra mi ser,
Yo sin su amor no soy nada.
Detén el tiempo en tus manos,
Haz esta noche perpetua,
Para que nunca se vaya de mí.
Para que nunca amanezca.
Para que nunca amanezca.
Para que nunca amanezca.

Canción mixteca

Qué lejos estoy del suelo donde he nacido,
Inmensa nostalgia invade mi pensamiento,
Y al verme tan solo y triste cual hoja al viento,
Quisiera llorar, quisiera morir
  de sentimiento. *(Repite)*

¡O tierra del sol!
suspiro por verte,
Ahora qué lejos
yo vivo sin luz, sin amor,
Y al verme tan solo y triste cual hoja al viento,
Quisiera llorar, quisiera morir
  de sentimiento.

El quelite

Qué bonito es el quelite
Bien haya quien lo sembró,
Que por sus orillas tiene
De quien acordarme yo.

Mañana me voy, mañana,
Mañana me voy de aquí.
Y el consuelo que me queda,
Que se han de acordar de mí.

Camino de San Ignacio
Me dio sueño y me dormí.
Y me despertó un gallito
Cantando quiquiriquí.

Mañana me voy, mañana,
Me voy por el nacional,
Adiós muchachas bonitas,
De esta hermosa capital.

Capítulo 1
Un amigo o una amiga

PRIMERA PARTE

Vocabulario   PALABRAS 1

Actividad A Listen and repeat.

Actividad B Listen and choose.

1. sí no	**3.** sí no	**5.** sí no
2. sí no	**4.** sí no	

Actividad C Listen and answer.

Vocabulario   PALABRAS 2

Actividad D Listen and repeat.

Actividad E Listen and choose.

1. a b c d e		**4.** a b c d e
2. a b c d e		**5.** a b c d e
3. a b c d e		

Actividad F Listen and choose.

1. a b c		**4.** a b c	
2. a b c		**5.** a b c	
3. a b c			

Estructura

Actividad A Listen and choose.

a   b

1. a b	**4.** a b	**7.** a b
2. a b	**5.** a b	**8.** a b
3. a b	**6.** a b	

Actividad B Listen.

Actividad C Listen and choose.

1.	**a.** Julia	**b.** Emilia	**c.** María
2.	**a.** Julio	**b.** Emilio	**c.** Marcos
3.	**a.** de Estados Unidos	**b.** de México	**c.** de Colombia

Actividad D Listen and choose.

1. a b c	**3.** a b c
2. a b c	**4.** a b c

Actividad E Listen and choose.

1. a b c

2. a b c

3. a b c

Conversación

Actividad F Listen.

Actividad G Listen and choose.

1. sí no   3. sí no   5. sí no   7. sí no

2. sí no   4. sí no   6. sí no   8. sí no

Pronunciación

Actividad H Pronunciación: *Las vocales a, o, u*

When you speak Spanish, it is important to pronounce the vowels carefully. The vowel sounds in Spanish are very short, clear, and concise. The vowels in English have several different pronunciations, but in Spanish they have only one sound. Imitate carefully the pronunciation of the vowels **a, o,** and **u**. Note that the pronunciation of **a** is similar to the *a* in *father*, **o** is similar to the *o* in *most*, and **u** is similar to the *u* in *flu*. Listen and repeat after the speaker.

a	o	u
Ana	o	uno
baja	no	mucha
amiga	Paco	mucho
alumna	amigo	muchacho

Ana es alumna.
Adán es alumno.
Ana es amiga de Adán.

Lectura

Actividad I Listen.

SEGUNDA PARTE

Actividad A   Listen and choose.

      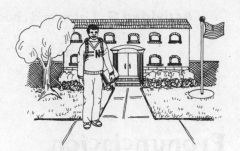

_____   _____   _____

_____   _____

Actividad B   Listen.

Actividad C   Write.

_____

_____

_____

Actividad D   Listen.

Actividad E   Listen and choose.

1. **a.** mexicana   **b.** colombiana   **c.** puertorriqueña

2. **a.** de San Juan   **b.** de San Jorge   **c.** de Barros

3. **a.** un colegio   **b.** la capital de   **c.** una isla
                                   Puerto Rico

4. **a.** una península   **b.** un continente   **c.** una isla

5. **a.** Es seria y   **b.** Es graciosa   **c.** Es alta y morena.
        ambiciosa.   y perezosa.

Capítulo 2
Alumnos y cursos

PRIMERA PARTE

Vocabulario   PALABRAS 1

Actividad A   Listen and repeat.

Actividad B   Listen and choose.

1. sí no		**3.** sí no		**5.** sí no		**7.** sí no	
2. sí no		**4.** sí no		**6.** sí no			

Actividad C   Listen and choose.

     1. a   b   c   **3.** a   b   c

     2. a   b   c   **4.** a   b   c

Vocabulario   PALABRAS 2

Actividad D   Listen and repeat.

Actividad E   Listen and match.

_____ intelligent   _____ interesting   _____ serious

_____ important   _____ popular

Actividad F   Listen and answer.

Actividad G Listen and choose.

1. **a.** aritmética   **b.** biología   **c.** historia
2. **a.** álgebra   **b.** arte   **c.** francés
3. **a.** cálculo   **b.** química   **c.** inglés
4. **a.** geografía   **b.** aritmética   **c.** latín
5. **a.** sociología   **b.** física   **c.** italiano
6. **a.** biología   **b.** educación física   **c.** español
7. **a.** historia   **b.** economía doméstica   **c.** arte

Estructura

Actividad A Listen and choose.

1.	1	2	**4.**	1	2	**7.**	1	2	**9.**	1	2
2.	1	2	**5.**	1	2	**8.**	1	2	**10.**	1	2
3.	1	2	**6.**	1	2					

Actividad B Listen and speak.

Actividad C Listen and choose.

1. a   b   c   4. a   b   c
2. a   b   c   5. a   b   c
3. a   b   c

Actividad D Listen and repeat.

Actividad E Listen and choose.

1. sí   no   3. sí   no
2. sí   no   4. sí   no

Actividad F Listen.

Actividad G   Listen and choose.

1. a   b   c   4. a   b   c

2. a   b   c   5. a   b   c

3. a   b   c

Actividad H   Listen and choose.

_____   _____   _____

   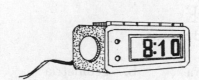   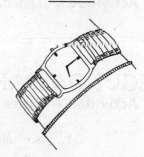

Conversación

Actividad I   Listen.

Actividad J   Listen and choose.

1. **a.** Coyoacán   **b.** San Antonio   **c.** San Francisco

2. **a.** Coyoacán   **b.** San Antonio   **c.** San Francisco

3. **a.** una parte de
       Tejas   **b.** una parte de la
                           Ciudad de México   **c.** una colonia de
                                                    España

4. **a.** Coyoacán   **b.** San Antonio   **c.** la Ciudad de México

Pronunciación

Actividad K Pronunciación: *Las vocales e, i*

The sounds of the Spanish vowels **e** and **i** are short, clear, and concise. The pronunciation of **e** is similar to *a* in *mate*. The pronunciation of **i** is similar to the *ee* in *bee* or *see*. Listen and repeat after the speaker.

e	i
Elena	Isabel
peso	Inés

Elena es una amiga de Felipe.
Inés es tímida.
Sí, Isabel es italiana.

Lectura

Actividad L Listen.

SEGUNDA PARTE

Actividad A Listen and choose.

1. **a.** álgebra   **b.** geometría   **c.** química

2. **a.** música   **b.** cálculo   **c.** arte

3. **a.** biología   **b.** español   **c.** historia

4. **a.** geografía   **b.** historia   **c.** aritmética

5. **a.** química   **b.** arte   **c.** historia

6. **a.** música   **b.** informática   **c.** educación física

Actividad B Look, listen, and answer.

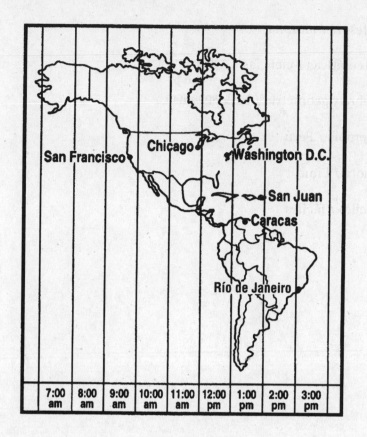

Actividad C Listen and choose.

1. Riobamba / Cochabamba

2. Bolivia / Venezuela

3. alumno / profesor

4. pública / privada

5. matemáticas / arte

Actividad D Listen and choose.

1. profesora / alumna

2. matemáticas / ciencias

3. álgebra y geometría / biología y física

4. Colombia / Perú

5. Bogotá / Lima

6. difíciles / fáciles

Capítulo 3
Las compras para la escuela

PRIMERA PARTE

Vocabulario PALABRAS 1

Actividad A Listen and repeat.

Actividad B Listen and choose.

_____ _____ _____

 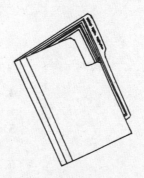 

_____ _____ _____

Actividad C Listen and choose.

_____ _____ _____ _____ _____

Vocabulario   PALABRAS 2

Actividad D Listen and repeat.

Actividad E Listen and choose.

   1. sí no   **3.** sí no   **5.** sí no

   2. sí no   **4.** sí no

Actividad F Listen and choose.

   1. a b c   **4.** a b c

   2. a b c   **5.** a b c

   3. a b c

Estructura

Actividad A Listen and answer.

Actividad B Listen and confirm.

Actividad C Listen and confirm.

Actividad D Listen.

Actividad E Listen and choose.

   1. a b c   **4.** a b c

   2. a b c   **5.** a b c

   3. a b c   **6.** a b c

Actividad F Listen and choose.

   1. a b c   **3.** a b c

   2. a b c   **4.** a b c

Conversación

Actividad G Listen.

Actividad H Listen and choose.

1. sí no   3. sí no   5. sí no

2. sí no   4. sí no   6. sí no

Pronunciación

Actividad I Pronunciación: *Las consonantes l, f, p, m, n*

The pronunciation of the consonants **l, f, p, m,** and **n** is very similar in both Spanish and English. However, the **p** is not followed by a puff of breath as it often is in English. Listen and repeat after the speaker.

Lolita es linda y elegante.
La falda de Felisa no es fea.
Paco es una persona popular.
La muchacha mexicana mira una goma.
Nando necesita un cuaderno nuevo.

Lectura

Actividad J Listen.

SEGUNDA PARTE

Actividad A Listen.

Actividad B Read and choose.

1. Where would this announcement be heard?

   a. stationery store   **b.** clothing store   **c.** cashier counter

2. What are they selling at a special offer?

   a. T-shirts   **b.** shirts   **c.** jackets

3. How much are they?

   a. 100 pesos   **b.** 50 pesos   **c.** 150 pesos

4. What choices are available?

   a. many colors and styles   **b.** many colors and prices   **c.** many colors and sizes

Actividad C   Listen and choose.

_____

_____   _____

AUDIO ACTIVITIES
Copyright © by The McGraw-Hill Companies, Inc.

Capítulo 4
En la escuela

PRIMERA PARTE

Vocabulario PALABRAS 1

Actividad A Listen and repeat.

Actividad B Listen and choose.

_____ _____ _____

_____ _____

Actividad C Listen and choose.

1. a   b   c   4. a   b   c

2. a   b   c   5. a   b   c

3. a   b   c

Vocabulario   PALABRAS 2

Actividad D Listen and repeat.

Actividad E Listen and choose.

1. sí   no   3. sí   no   5. sí   no   7. sí   no

2. sí   no   4. sí   no   6. sí   no   8. sí   no

Actividad F Listen and choose.

_____

_____

_____

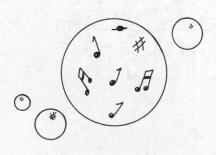

_____

_____

_____

Estructura

Actividad A Listen.

Actividad B Listen and choose.

1. **a.** Llegan   **b.** Enseñan   **c.** Cantan

2. **a.** Escuchan   **b.** Van   **c.** Hablan

3. **a.** Prestan   **b.** Cuestan   **c.** Estudian

4. **a.** Toman   **b.** Prestan   **c.** Sacan

5. **a.** Sacan   **b.** Llegan   **c.** Toman

Actividad C Listen and answer.

Actividad D Listen and choose.

1. a   b   c   4. a   b   c

2. a   b   c   5. a   b   c

3. a   b   c   6. a   b   c

Actividad E Listen and answer.

1. la fiesta   4. sí

2. a pie   5. Sara

3. Marta y Sara   6. bien

Conversación

Actividad F Listen.

Actividad G Listen and choose.

1. a   b   c   4. a   b   c

2. a   b   c   5. a   b   c

3. a   b   c

Pronunciación

Actividad H Pronunciación: *La consonante t*

The **t** in Spanish is pronounced with the tip of the tongue pressed against the upper teeth. It is not followed by a puff of air. Listen and repeat after the speaker.

ta	te	ti	to	tu
taco	Teresa	tienda	toma	tú
canta	interesante	tiempo	tomate	estudia
está	casete	latín	Juanito	estupendo

Tito necesita siete disquetes de la tienda.
Tú tomas apuntes en latín.
Teresa invita a Tito a la fiesta.

Lectura

Actividad I Listen.

Segunda parte

Actividad A Listen.

Actividad B Listen and choose.

1. **a.** Mercedes   **b.** Jorge   **c.** Leonor

2. **a.** Mercedes   **b.** Jorge   **c.** Leonor

3. **a.** Mercedes   **b.** Jorge   **c.** Leonor

4. **a.** a la tienda   **b.** a casa   **c.** a la escuela

5. **a.** Mercedes   **b.** Jorge   **c.** Leonor

6. **a.** a casa de Leonor   **b.** a la tienda   **c.** a casa de Jorge

7. **a.** para estudiar   **b.** para mirar la tele   **c.** para bailar

8. **a.** discos   **b.** meriendas   **c.** casetes

9. **a.** discos   **b.** meriendas   **c.** casetes

Nombre _____ Fecha _____

Actividad C Listen and choose.

a

b

c

d

e

f

g

h

_____ **1.** Pablo

_____ **2.** María

_____ **3.** Susana

_____ **4.** Roberto

_____ **5.** Beatriz

_____ **6.** Fernando

_____ **7.** Elena

_____ **8.** Carlos

Actividad D Listen and choose.

INLINGUA

TARIFAS

San Juan—Ponce

$1.050

Incluye:

— Viaje NYC—Puerto Rico—NYC.

— 10 días alojamiento en familias pensión completa.

— Actividades todas las tardes.

— Asistencia permanente de nuestro equipo de profesores y monitores.

— Seguro de accidentes y de asistencia médica.

— 20 horas de clase.

— Clases de cuatro personas.

— Fiesta de despedida y bienvenida.

1. sí no   **3.** sí no   **5.** sí no   **7.** sí no

2. sí no   **4.** sí no   **6.** sí no   **8.** sí no

Capítulo 5
En el café

PRIMERA PARTE

Vocabulario   PALABRAS 1

Actividad A   Listen and repeat.

Actividad B   Listen and choose.

	Para comer	Para beber			Para comer	Para beber
1.	_____	_____		6.	_____	_____
2.	_____	_____		7.	_____	_____
3.	_____	_____		8.	_____	_____
4.	_____	_____		9.	_____	_____
5.	_____	_____		10.	_____	_____

Actividad C   Listen and choose.

_____   _____   _____

_____   _____

Actividad D Listen and choose.

1. a   b   c   4. a   b   c

2. a   b   c   5. a   b   c

3. a   b   c

Actividad E Listen and repeat.

Actividad F Listen and repeat.

Actividad G Listen.

Actividad H Listen and choose.

1. sí   no   3. sí   no   5. sí   no

2. sí   no   4. sí   no   6. sí   no

Vocabulario   PALABRAS 2

Actividad I Listen and repeat.

Actividad J Listen and repeat.

Actividad K Listen and choose.

	Vegetal	Fruta			Vegetal	Fruta
1.	_____	_____		5.	_____	_____
2.	_____	_____		6.	_____	_____
3.	_____	_____		7.	_____	_____
4.	_____	_____		8.	_____	_____

Actividad L Listen and choose.

_____   _____   _____   _____

_____   _____   _____   _____

Estructura

Actividad A Listen and speak.

Actividad B Listen and speak.

Actividad C Listen and choose.

1. a b c   4. a b c

2. a b c   5. a b c

3. a b c   6. a b c

Conversación

Actividad D Listen.

Actividad E Listen and choose.

1. sí no   3. sí no   5. sí no   7. sí no

2. sí no   4. sí no   6. sí no   8. sí no

Pronunciación

Actividad F Pronunciación: *La consonante d*

The pronunciation of **d** in Spanish varies according to its position in the word. When a word begins with **d** (initial position) or follows the consonants **l** or **n,** the tongue gently strikes the back of the upper front teeth. Listen and repeat after the speaker.

da	de	di	do	du
da	dependiente	difícil	domingo	dulce
merienda	vende	andino	condominio	

When **d** appears within the word between vowels (medial position), **d** is extremely soft. Your tongue should strike the lower part of your upper teeth, almost between the upper and lower teeth. Listen and repeat after the speaker.

da	de	di	do	du
privada	modelo	estudio	helado	educación
ensalada	cuaderno	medio	congelado	

When a word ends in **d** (final position), **d** is either extremely soft or omitted completely—not pronounced. Listen and repeat after the speaker.

nacionalidad   ciudad

Diego da el disco compacto a Donato en la ciudad.
El dependiente vende helado y limonada.
Adela compra la merienda en la tienda.

Lectura

Actividad G Listen.

SEGUNDA PARTE
Actividad A Listen and choose.

	Papelería	Zapatería	Supermercado	Mercado	Café
1.	_____	_____	_____	_____	_____
2.	_____	_____	_____	_____	_____
3.	_____	_____	_____	_____	_____
4.	_____	_____	_____	_____	_____
5.	_____	_____	_____	_____	_____

Actividad B Listen and choose.

_____

_____

_____

_____

Actividad C Look, listen, and choose.

1. **a.** 1   **b.** 9

2. **a.** el almuerzo   **b.** el desayuno

3. **a.** la comida   **b.** el desayuno

4. **a.** de lunes a jueves   **b.** lunes y jueves

5. **a.** sí   **b.** no

6. **a.** sí   **b.** no

7. **a.** no   **b.** sí

Capítulo 6
La familia y su casa

PRIMERA PARTE

Vocabulario   PALABRAS 1

Actividad A Listen and repeat.

Actividad B Listen and choose.

La familia Moliner

Verónica

Felipe

1. sí no	4. sí no	7. sí no	10. sí no
2. sí no	5. sí no	8. sí no	
3. sí no	6. sí no	9. sí no	

Actividad C Listen and choose.

1. **a.** tío   **b.** hermano   **c.** abuelo

2. **a.** tío   **b.** primo   **c.** sobrino

3. **a.** tía   **b.** prima   **c.** sobrina

4. **a.** abuelos   **b.** primos   **c.** sobrinos

5. **a.** prima   **b.** sobrina   **c.** tía

6. **a.** abuelo   **b.** sobrino   **c.** tío

7. **a.** abuela   **b.** tía   **c.** prima

8. **a.** sobrino   **b.** abuelo   **c.** tío

9. **a.** tíos   **b.** abuelos   **c.** sobrinos

Actividad D Listen and choose.

1. a b c   **2.** a b c   **3.** a b c   **4.** a b c

Vocabulario   PALABRAS 2

Actividad E Listen and repeat.

Actividad F Listen and choose.

_____   _____   _____

_____   _____   _____

Actividad G Listen and choose.

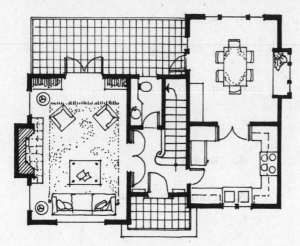

La planta baja

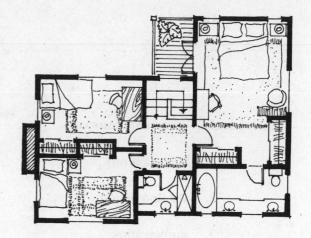

el primer piso

1. **a.** cuatro   **b.** seis

2. **a.** cuatro   **b.** cinco

3. **a.** planta baja   **b.** primer piso

4. **a.** planta baja   **b.** primer piso

5. **a.** planta baja   **b.** primer piso

6. **a.** planta baja   **b.** primer piso

Actividad H Listen and speak.

Estructura

Actividad A Listen.

Actividad B Listen and choose.

1. sí no   3. sí no   5. sí no

2. sí no   4. sí no

Actividad C Listen and choose.

1. a b c

2. a b c

3. a b c

4. a b c

5. a b c

6. a b c

Actividad D Listen and answer.

1. buenas notas

2. ver una película

3. quince años

4. una A

5. comprar la casa

Actividad E Listen and answer.

1. a las ocho

2. el lunes

3. a las cuatro y media

4. Teresa

5. a mi abuela

Actividad F Listen and answer.

1. preparar la comida

2. escribir una composición

3. sacar buenas notas

4. escuchar al profesor

5. trabajar

Actividad G Listen and answer.

Conversación

Actividad H Listen.

Actividad I Listen and choose.

1. a b c

2. a b c

3. a b c

4. a b c

Pronunciación

Actividad J   Pronunciación: *Las consonantes b, v*

There is no difference in pronunciation between a **b** and a **v** in Spanish. The **b** or **v** sound is somewhat softer than the sound of an English *b*. When making this sound, the lips barely touch. Listen and repeat after the speaker.

ba	be	bi	bo	bu
bajo	bebé	bicicleta	bonito	bueno
bastante	escribe	bien	recibo	bus
trabaja	recibe	biología	árbol	aburrido

va	ve	vi	vo	vu
vamos	verano	vive	vosotros	vuelo
nueva	venezolano	violín	voleibol	

El joven vive en la Avenida Bolívar en Bogotá.
Bárbara trabaja los sábados en el laboratorio de biología.
La joven ve la bicicleta nueva en la televisión.

Lectura

Actividad K   Listen.

SEGUNDA PARTE

Actividad A   Listen.

Actividad B   Listen and choose.

1. What's the offer for?

   a.   a house   b.   an apartment   c.   an apartment
                                                             building

2. Where is it located?

   a.   in the suburbs   b.   on a main street   c.   in the city center

3. What floor is it on?

   a.   the ground floor   b.   the second   c.   the twentieth

4. How many rooms does it have?

   a.   3   b.   7   c.   20

5. What's so exceptional about it?

   a.   It has a modern   b.   It has several   c.   It has a private
        kitchen.   balconies.   elevator.

6. How can you get more information?

    a. Visit the place.
    b. Call the real estate agency.
    c. Go to Avenida Simón Bolívar.

7. What city is the apartment in?

    a. Benavides
    b. Bolívar
    c. Bogotá

Actividad C Listen.

Actividad D Listen and choose.

1. **a.** una escuela   **b.** un restaurante   **c.** un baile
2. **a.** para celebrar y comer   **b.** para leer y escribir   **c.** para estudiar
3. **a.** a unos kilómetros del centro de la ciudad   **b.** en el centro de la ciudad   **c.** en un parque
4. **a.** a 6 kilómetros   **b.** a 16 kilómetros   **c.** a 60 kilómetros
5. **a.** en la planta baja   **b.** en los jardines   **c.** en la cocina
6. **a.** 30   **b.** 50   **c.** 70
7. **a.** la cocina   **b.** el comedor   **c.** el banquete
8. **a.** dos   **b.** cuatro   **c.** ocho
9. **a.** dos a tres   **b.** cuatro a ocho   **c.** seis a diez
10. **a.** Montes   **b.** Ruano   **c.** Rojas
11. **a.** una escuela   **b.** el Edificio Ruano   **c.** un jardín
12. **a.** lunes   **b.** martes   **c.** domingo

Capítulo 7
Deportes de equipo

PRIMERA PARTE

Vocabulario — PALABRAS 1

Actividad A Listen and repeat.

Actividad B Listen and choose.

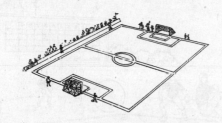

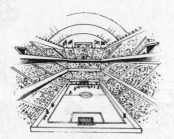

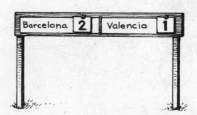

Actividad C Listen and choose.

Actividad D Listen and choose.

1. sí no   3. sí no   5. sí no

2. sí no   4. sí no

Vocabulario   PALABRAS 2

Actividad E Listen and repeat.

Actividad F Listen and choose.

Actividad G Listen and repeat.

Actividad H Listen and choose.

_____   _____   _____   _____

Actividad I   Listen and choose.

	El béisbol	El fútbol	El básquetbol
1.	_____	_____	_____
2.	_____	_____	_____
3.	_____	_____	_____
4.	_____	_____	_____
5.	_____	_____	_____
6.	_____	_____	_____
7.	_____	_____	_____
8.	_____	_____	_____

Actividad J   Listen and choose.

1. a   b   c   4. a   b   c

2. a   b   c   5. a   b   c

3. a   b   c   6. a   b   c

Estructura

Actividad A   Listen and answer.

Actividad B   Listen and speak.

Actividad C   Listen and choose.

1. a   b   c   4. a   b   c

2. a   b   c   5. a   b   c

3. a   b   c   6. a   b   c

Actividad D   Listen and speak.

Actividad E   Listen and choose.

1. sí   no   2. sí   no   3. sí   no   4. sí   no

Actividad F   Listen and speak.

Conversación

Actividad G Listen.

Actividad H Listen and choose.

1.	sí no	**3.**	sí no	**5.**	sí no
2.	sí no	**4.**	sí no	**6.**	sí no

Pronunciación

Actividad I Pronunciación: *Las consonantes s, c, z*

The consonant **s** is pronounced the same as the *s* in *sing*. Listen and repeat after the speaker.

sa	se	si	so	su
sala	base	sí	peso	su
pasa	serio	simpático	sopa	Susana
saca	seis	siete	sobrino	

The consonant **c** in combination with **e** or **i** (**ce, ci**) is pronounced the same as an **s** in all areas of Latin America. In many parts of Spain, **ce** and **ci** are pronounced like **th** in English. Likewise, the pronunciation of **z** in combination with **a, o, u** (**za, zo, zu**) is the same as an **s** throughout Latin American and as a **th** in most areas of Spain. Listen and repeat after the speaker.

za	ce	ci	zo	zu
cabeza	cero	cinco	zona	zumo
empieza	encesta	ciudad	almuerzo	Zúñiga

González enseña en la sala de clase.
El sobrino de Susana es serio y sincero.
La ciudad tiene cinco zonas.
Toma el almuerzo a las doce y diez en la cocina.

Lectura

Actividad J Listen.

Segunda parte

Actividad A Listen.

Actividad B Listen and choose.

1. Es un partido de _____.

   a. baloncesto   **b.** béisbol   **c.** fútbol

2. Los dos equipos son Madrid y _____.

   a. Real   **b.** Barcelona   **c.** Vargas

3. Quedan _____ minutos en el segundo tiempo.

   a. dos   **b.** tres   **c.** cuatro

4. Vargas lanza el balón con _____.

   a. la cabeza   **b.** el pic   **c.** la mano

5. Meten un gol en el _____ minuto del partido.

   a. primer   **b.** tercer   **c.** último

6. El resultado del partido es _____.

   a. una victoria   **b.** un juego   **c.** que Vargas pierde
       para Madrid   empatado

Actividad C Listen.

Actividad D Listen and answer.

1. Where are the famous archeological ruins in Honduras?

_____

2. In what country is Chichen Itzá?

_____

3. Where were there recent digs in Puerto Rico?

_____

4. What's the name of an Indian tribe in Puerto Rico?

_____

5. What game did they play?

_____

Actividad E Listen and choose.

1. a   b   c

2. a   b   c

3. a   b   c

Capítulo 8
La salud y el médico

PRIMERA PARTE

Vocabulario   PALABRAS 1

Actividad A Listen and repeat.

Actividad B Listen and choose.

____ ____ ____   ____ ____ ____

Actividad C Listen and choose.

1. a b c   4. a b c

2. a b c   5. a b c

3. a b c

Vocabulario   PALABRAS 2

Actividad D Listen and repeat.

Actividad E Listen and choose.

1. sí no   3. sí no   5. sí no

2. sí no   4. sí no   6. sí no

Actividad F Listen and choose.

1. sí no   3. sí no   5. sí no
2. sí no   4. sí no   6. sí no

Estructura

Actividad A Listen and answer.

1. alto y rubio
2. simpáticos
3. no, antipática
4. sí
5. grande y moderna

6. González
7. inteligente y simpático(a)
8. interesante
9. difícil

Actividad B Listen and answer.

1. enfermo
2. bien
3. aburridos
4. cansados

5. triste
6. no, tranquilos
7. contenta

Actividad C Listen and create.

1. la médica / inteligente
2. su consulta / moderna
3. el enfermo / simpático
4. la muchacha / enferma

5. la consulta / en el edificio Burgos
6. el edificio / alto
7. el paciente / en el hospital
8. el hospital / viejo

Actividad D Listen and choose.

	Location	Origin		Location	Origin
1.	☐	☐	6.	☐	☐
2.	☐	☐	7.	☐	☐
3.	☐	☐	8.	☐	☐
4.	☐	☐	9.	☐	☐
5.	☐	☐	10.	☐	☐

Actividad E Listen.

Actividad F Listen and choose.

	Characteristic	**Condition**	**Origin**	**Location**
1.	☐	☐	☐	☐
2.	☐	☐	☐	☐
3.	☐	☐	☐	☐
4.	☐	☐	☐	☐
5.	☐	☐	☐	☐
6.	☐	☐	☐	☐
7.	☐	☐	☐	☐
8.	☐	☐	☐	☐
9.	☐	☐	☐	☐

Actividad G Listen and answer.

1. el médico

2. la cabeza

3. la médica

4. unas pastillas

5. no

6. el médico

7. el farmacéutico

Conversación

Actividad H Listen.

Actividad I Listen and choose.

1. a b   3. a b   5. a b

2. a b   4. a b   6. a b

Pronunciación

Actividad J Pronunciación: *La consonante c*

You have already learned that **c** in combination with **e** or **i (ce, ci)** is pronounced like an **s**. The consonant **c** in combination with **a, o, u (ca, co, cu)** has a hard **k** sound. Since **ce, ci** have the soft **s** sound, **c** changes to **qu** when it combines with **e** or **i (que, qui)** in order to maintain the hard **k** sound. Listen and repeat after the speaker.

ca   que   qui   co   cu
cama   que   equipo   como   cubano
casa   queso   aquí   médico
catarro   parque   química   cocina
cansado   pequeño   tranquilo
cabeza
boca

El médico cubano está en la consulta pequeña.
El queso está en la cocina de la casa.
El cubano come el queso aquí en el parque pequeño.

Lectura

Actividad K Listen.

SEGUNDA PARTE

Actividad A Listen.

Actividad B Listen and complete.

1. The ad is for people with _____.

2. The name of the product being advertised is _____.

3. It can be obtained in a _____.

4. It comes in the form of _____.

5. It is available in _____ sizes.

6. It's really good for _____.

Actividad C Listen.

Actividad D Listen and write.

_____

_____

Actividad E Listen and speak.

Capítulo 9
El verano y el invierno

PRIMERA PARTE

Vocabulario   PALABRAS 1

Actividad A Listen and repeat.

Actividad B Listen and choose.

_____   _____   _____

_____   _____

Actividad C Listen and choose.

1. sí no	**4.** sí no	**7.** sí no	**10.** sí no
2. sí no	**5.** sí no	**8.** sí no	
3. sí no	**6.** sí no	**9.** sí no	

Vocabulario   PALABRAS 2

Actividad D Listen and repeat.

Actividad E Listen and choose.

1. _____   _____   2. _____   _____

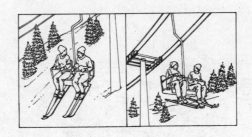

3. _____   _____   4. _____   _____

5. _____   _____

Actividad F Listen and choose.

	Verano	Invierno			Verano	Invierno
1.	_____	_____		6.	_____	_____
2.	_____	_____		7.	_____	_____
3.	_____	_____		8.	_____	_____
4.	_____	_____		9.	_____	_____
5.	_____	_____		10.	_____	_____

Estructura

Actividad A Listen and choose.

	Presente	Pasado	Presente y pasado		Presente	Pasado	Presente y pasado
1.	_____	_____	_____	6.	_____	_____	_____
2.	_____	_____	_____	7.	_____	_____	_____
3.	_____	_____	_____	8.	_____	_____	_____
4.	_____	_____	_____	9.	_____	_____	_____
5.	_____	_____	_____	10.	_____	_____	_____

Actividad B Listen and answer.

1. la playa

2. 1:00

3. sí

4. una toalla, la crema protectora

5. sí

6. sí, Laura

7. no

Actividad C Listen and answer.

Actividad D Listen and speak.

Conversación

Actividad E Listen.

Actividad F Listen and choose.

1. sí no   3. sí no   5. sí no   7. sí no

2. sí no   4. sí no   6. sí no

Pronunciación

Actividad G Pronunciación: *La consonante g*

The consonant **g** has two sounds, hard and soft. You will study the soft sound in Chapter 10. **G** in combination with **a, o, u (ga, go, gu)** is pronounced somewhat like the **g** in the English word *go*. To maintain this hard **g** sound with **e** or **i**, a **u** is placed after the **g: gue, gui.** Listen and repeat after the speaker.

ga	gue	gui	go	gu
gafa	Rodríguez	guitarra	goma	agua
amiga	guerrilla	guía	estómago	guante
garganta			tengo	
paga			juego	
gato				

El gato no juega en el agua.
Juego béisbol con el guante de mi amigo Rodríguez.
No tengo la guitarra de Gómez.

Lectura

Actividad H Listen.

Segunda Parte

Actividad A Listen.

Actividad B Listen and choose.

1. What is this ad for?

   a. ski trips   **b.** skating lessons   **c.** sportswear

2. For how many days is the stay at the resort?

   a. 4   **b.** 8   **c.** 12

3. What is the destination?

   a. Buenos Aires   **b.** Córdoba   **c.** Bariloche

4. How many departures are there per week?

   a. 2   **b.** 4   **c.** 8

5. What is the means of transportation?

   a. bus   **b.** train   **c.** plane

6. What is the price?

   a. 500 pesos   **b.** 5,000 pesos   **c.** 15,000 pesos

7. What is the address of the agency?

    a. Córdoba 81   **b.** Buenos Aires 80   **c.** Gorostiza 88

8. What is their phone number?

    a. 312-69-75   **b.** 312-67-59   **c.** 312-77-69

Actividad C Listen.

Actividad D Listen and choose.

1. ¿Para quienes es el anuncio?

    a. para personas que quieren trabajo

    b. para enfermos

    c. para personas que van de vacaciones

2. ¿Cual es el nombre del lugar que anuncian?

    a. Palmas del Mar

    b. Vistas del mar

    c. San Juan

3. ¿Dónde está el lugar?

    a. en un lago

    b. en las montañas

    c. en la costa

4. ¿Qué deporte no menciona el anuncio?

    a. el esquí acuático

    b. el golf

    c. el tenis

5. ¿Qué pueden hacer las personas que no quieren hacer deportes?

    a. tomar el sol

    b. ir a San Juan

    c. esquiar

6. ¿A cuántos kilómetros de San Juan está?

    a. cuatro

    b. catorce

    c. cuarenta

Actividad E Listen.

Actividad F Listen and write.

1. What kind of product is being advertised?

    _____

2. What is the name of the product?

    _____

3. Where should you take it?

    _____

4. What will it do for you?

    _____

5. How much does it cost?

    _____

Actividad G Listen and choose.

1. **a.** prices   **b.** the weather   **c.** hours

2. **a.** transportation   **b.** facilities   **c.** rooms

3. **a.** lessons   **b.** the weather   **c.** food

4. **a.** rooms   **b.** hours   **c.** transportation

5. **a.** the weather   **b.** prices   **c.** hours

6. **a.** food   **b.** transportation   **c.** lessons

7. **a.** rooms   **b.** facilities   **c.** prices

8. **a.** facilities   **b.** lessons   **c.** prices

9. **a.** facilities   **b.** the weather   **c.** prices

Capítulo 10
Diversiones culturales

PRIMERA PARTE

Vocabulario   PALABRAS 1

Actividad A Listen and repeat.

Actividad B Listen and choose.

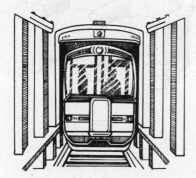

Actividad C Listen and choose.

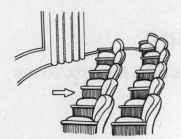  

———   ———   ———

———   ———   ———

Actividad D Listen and choose.

1. a b c   4. a b c

2. a b c   5. a b c

3. a b c

Vocabulario   PALABRAS 2

Actividad E Listen and repeat.

Actividad F Listen and choose.

1. a b   3. a b   5. a b

2. a b   4. a b   6. a b

Actividad G Listen and choose.

1.	a	b	c		**4.**	a	b	c
2.	a	b	c		**5.**	a	b	c
3.	a	b	c		**6.**	a	b	c

Estructura

Actividad A Listen and answer.

Actividad B Listen and choose.

1.	pasado	presente		**5.**	pasado	presente
2.	pasado	presente		**6.**	pasado	presente
3.	pasado	presente		**7.**	pasado	presente
4.	pasado	presente		**8.**	pasado	presente

Actividad C Listen and choose.

1.	a	b	c		**4.**	a	b	c
2.	a	b	c		**5.**	a	b	c
3.	a	b	c		**6.**	a	b	c

Actividad D Listen and speak.

Actividad E Listen and answer.

1. sí

2. las noticias

3. sí

4. sí

5. no, hablar

Conversación

Actividad F Listen.

Actividad G Listen and choose.

1. sí no   4. sí no   7. sí no

2. sí no   5. sí no   8. sí no

3. sí no   6. sí no   9. sí no

Pronunciación

Actividad H Pronunciación: *Las consonantes j y g*

The Spanish **j** sound does not exist in English. In Spain, the **j** sound is very guttural. It comes from the throat. In Latin America, the **j** sound is much softer. Listen and repeat after the speaker.

ja	je	ji	jo	ju
Jaime	Jesús	Jiménez	joven	jugar
hija	garaje	ají	viejo	junio
roja			trabajo	julio
			ojos	

G in combination with **e** or **i** (**ge, gi**) has the same sound as **j**. For this reason you must pay particular attention to the spelling of the words with **je, ji, ge,** and **gi.** Listen and repeat after the speaker.

ge	gi
general	biología
gente	alergia
generoso	original
Insurgentes	

El hijo del viejo general José trabaja en junio en Gijón.
El jugador juega en el gimnasio.
El joven Jaime toma jugo de naranja.

Lectura

Actividad I Listen.

Segunda parte

Actividad A Listen and write.

1. What kind of radio broadcast is it?

    _____

2. When was the first performance?

    _____

3. What is the title?

    _____

4. Who is Guillermo Sampere?

    _____

5. What happened to Angelito?

    _____

Actividad B Look, listen, and answer.

Bodas de sangre

Director	Alonso Hernández
Actores	Sandra Arniches / Conrado Herrera
Sesiones	martes y miercoles 8:00 P.M.
	jueves 2:00 P.M. y 8:00 P.M.
	sábado 3:00 P.M. y 9:00 P.M.
	domingo 2:00 P.M. y 8:00 P.M.
	lunes descanso, no hay función

¡NO HAY ENTRADAS PARA ESTE SÁBADO!

Precios	Butacas de patio, filas 1–11 500 pesos
	Butacas de patio, filas 12–26 300 pesos
	Balcones 150 pesos

Actividad C Listen and write.

1. _____

2. _____

3. _____

4. _____

5. _____

Capítulo 11
Un viaje en avión

PRIMERA PARTE

Vocabulario   PALABRAS 1

Actividad A Listen and repeat.

Actividad B Listen and choose.

      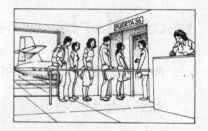

_____   _____   _____

_____   _____

Actividad C Listen and repeat.

Actividad D Look, listen, and answer.

Vocabulario   PALABRAS 2

Actividad E Listen and repeat.

Actividad F Listen and choose.

1. a b c   4. a b c

2. a b c   5. a b c

3. a b c   6. a b c

Actividad G Listen and choose.

1. sí no   3. sí no   5. sí no

2. sí no   4. sí no   6. sí no

Estructura

Actividad A Listen and answer.

Actividad B Listen and answer.

1. sí

2. un viaje

3. sí

4. la ropa

5. sí, libros

6. refrescos

7. a las cuatro

Actividad C Listen and answer.

1. sí   2. sí   3. sí   4. no   5. no

Actividad D Listen and answer.

Actividad E Listen and answer.

1. estudiar

2. trabajar

3. escribir

4. aterrizar

5. inspeccionar el equipaje

6. abrir la maleta

Conversación

Actividad F Listen.

Actividad G Listen and choose.

1. a b c

2. a b c

3. a b c

4. a b c

5. a b c

6. a b c

7. a b c

Pronunciación

Actividad H Pronunciación: *La consonante r*

When a word begins with an **r** (initial position), the **r** is trilled in Spanish. Within a word **rr** is also trilled. The Spanish trilled **r** does not exist in English. Listen and repeat after the speaker.

ra	re	ri	ro	ru
rápido	reclama	Ricardo	Roberto	Rubén
raqueta	recoger	rico	rojo	rubio
párrafo	receta	perrito	perro	
	corre	aterrizar	catarro	
			carro	

The sound for a single **r** within a word (medial positon) does not exist in English either. It is trilled less than the initial **r** or **rr**. Repeat after the speaker.

ra	re	ri	ro	ru
demora	arena	Clarita	maletero	Perú
verano		consultorio	número	Aruba
para			miro	

El mesero recoge los refrescos.
El perrito de Rubén corre en la arena.
El maletero corre rápido por el aeropuerto.
El avión para Puerto Rico aterriza con una demora de una hora.
El rico tiene una raqueta en el carro.

Lectura

Actividad I   Listen.

SEGUNDA PARTE

Actividad A Listen and choose.

Validez Validity	Días Days	Salida Dep.	Llegada Arrival	Nº vuelo Flight No.	Vía Vía	Avión/Clase Aircraft/Class
VALENCIA *(Cont.)*						
LA CORUÑA *(Cont.)*						
09 Abr / 28 Jun	12345	12.40	16.20	IB0333/**AO126**	MAD	757/M88/CYL
	12345 7	15.30	19.15	IB0349/**AO130**	MAD	32S/DC9/CYL
/ 12 Jul	12345	18.25	21.30	IB0339/**AO128**	MAD	757/M88/CYL
02 Sep /	12345	18.25	21.30	IB0339/**AO128**	MAD	757/M88/CYL
LANZAROTE						
25 Jun / 30 Sep	123 56	07.45	11.15	IB0323/**AO169**	MAD	757/M88/CYL
/ 24 Jun	1 3 5	07.45	11.15	IB0323/**AO169**	MAD	757/M88/CYL
02 Oct	1 3 5	07.45	11.15	IB0323/**AO169**	MAD	757/M88/CYL
	4 67	08.05-	11.35	IB1343/**AO761**	BCN	757/DC9/CYL
02 Sep /	12345	08.35	13.15	IB0327/**AO157**	MAD	32S/M88/CYL
11 Abr / 28 Jun	12345	08.35	13.15	IB0327/**AO157**	MAD	32S/M88/CYL
/ 10 Abr	123	08.35	13.15	IB0327/**AO157**	MAD	32S/M88/CYL
MENORCA						
	1234567	08.10	11.10	**AO492/AO630**	PMI	DC9/CYL
	12345 7	19.10	21.50	IB1347/**AO211**	BCN	M87/DC9/CYL
PALMA MALLORCA						
	1234567	08.10	08.50	**AO492**		DC9/CYL
	1 3 5 7	14.05	14.45	**AO494**		DC9/CYL
	2 4 6	14.05	14.45	**AO552**		DC9/CYL
	1234	17.40	18.20	**AO496**		DC9/CYL
	1234567	20.55	21.35	**AO498**		DC9/CYL
PAMPLONA						
	12345 7	15.30	17.50	IB0349/**AO604**	MAD	32S/M88/CYL
SAN SEBASTIAN						
02 Sep /	12345	12.40	17.10	IB0333/**AO110**	MAD	757/M88/CYL
09 Abr / 28 Jun	12345	12.40	17.10	IB0333/**AO110**	MAD	757/M88/CYL
SANTA CRUZ DE LA PALMA						
	2 4 6	07.45	12.55	IB0323/**AO165**	MAD	757/DC9/CYL
03 Sep /	2 4	08.35	12.55	IB0327/**AO165**	MAD	32S/DC9/CYL
11 Abr / 27 Jun	2 4	08.35	12.55	IB0327/**AO165**	MAD	32S/DC9/CYL
SANTANDER						
02 Sep / 27 Sep	1 3 5	08.35	12.30	IB0327/**AO134**	MAD	32S/DC9/CYL
	12345 7	15.30	19.30	IB0349/**AO136**	MAD	32S/M88/CYL

Validez Validity	Días Days	Salida Dep.	Llegada Arrival	Nº vuelo Flight No.	Vía Vía	Avión/Clase Aircraft/Class
VALENCIA *(Cont.)*						
VIGO						
	12345	07.45	10.40	IB0323/**AO270**	MAD	757/M88/CYL
02 Sep /	12345	12.40	15.15	IB0333/**AO264**	MAD	757/DC9/CYL
09 Abr / 28 Jun	12345	12.40	15.15	IB0333/**AO264**	MAD	757/DC9/CYL
/ 12 Jul	12345	18.25	21.30	IB0339/**AO268**	MAD	757/M88/CYL
02 Sep /	12345	18.25	21.30	IB0339/**AO268**	MAD	757/M88/CYL
ZARAGOZA						
	12345 7	15.30	19.30	IB0349/**AO760**	MAD	32S/DC9/CYL
VALLADOLID (VLL) a/to ☎ IB 901333111						
BARCELONA						
	12345 7	17.15	18.20	**AO726**		M88/CYL
IBIZA						
	12345 7	17.15	21.45	**AO726/AO245**	BCN	M88/CYL
MENORCA						
	12345 7	17.15	20.40	**AO726/AO209**	BCN	M88/DC9/CYL
PALMA MALLORCA						
	12345 7	17.15	20.00	**AO726/IB1736**	BCN	M88/72S/CYL
PARIS (ORLY SUD APT)						
	12345	14.45	16.30	**AO964**		M88/CYL
VIGO						
	12345	19.45	20.25	**AO965**		M88/CYL
VIGO (VGO) a/to ☎ AO (986)487625/26						
ALICANTE						
	1234567	07.30	11.55	**AO259/AO642**	MAD	M88/CYL
	12345	11.50	15.25	**AO271/AO644**	MAD	M88/CYL
	12345 7	15.55	19.55	**AO265/AO646**	MAD	DC9/M88/CYL
	1234567	18.35	22.50	**AO267/AO648**	MAD	M88/CYL

1. sí no   3. sí no   5. sí no   7. sí no

2. sí no   4. sí no   6. sí no   8. sí no

Actividad B Listen.

Actividad C Listen and choose.

1. Who is speaking?

   a. the pilot
   b. the flight attendant
   c. the airport announcer

2. What is the destination?

   a. North Carolina
   b. Caracas
   c. Buenos Aires

3. About how many hours is the flight?

   a. 7
   b. 9
   c. 12

4. At what time will they land?

   a. 9:10 A.M.
   b. 11:00 A.M.
   c. 12:20 P.M.

5. At what altitude are they?

   a. 1,100 meters
   b. 11,000 meters
   c. 111,000 meters

6. What is their air speed?

   a. 120 kph
   b. 1,200 kph
   c. 12,000 kph

7. In what direction are they flying?

   a. north
   b. south
   c. west

8. What countries will they fly over?

   a. Brazil and Uruguay
   b. Chile and Bolivia
   c. Spain and Portugal

9. How many flight attendants are on board?

   a. 12
   b. 18
   c. 20

Capítulo 12
Una gira

PRIMERA PARTE

Vocabulario   PALABRAS 1

Actividad A Listen and repeat.

Actividad B Listen and choose.

_____   _____   _____

_____   _____   _____

_____   _____   _____

Actividad C Listen and choose.

1. sí no   3. sí no   5. sí no   7. sí no

2. sí no   4. sí no   6. sí no   8. sí no

Actividad D Listen and choose.

1. sí no   3. sí no   5. sí no

2. sí no   4. sí no

Vocabulario   PALABRAS 2

Actividad E Listen and repeat.

Actividad F Listen and choose.

_____

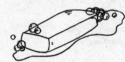
_____

_____

_____

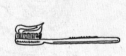
_____

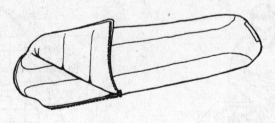
_____

Actividad G Listen and choose.

1. sí no   3. sí no   5. sí no

2. sí no   4. sí no   6. sí no

Estructura

Actividad A Listen and answer.

Actividad B Listen and answer.

Actividad C Listen and choose.

1. a   b   c   3. a   b   c

2. a   b   c   4. a   b   c

Conversación

Actividad D Listen.

Actividad E Listen and choose.

1. sí   no   3. sí   no   5. sí   no   7. sí   no

2. sí   no   4. sí   no   6. sí   no   8. sí   no

Pronunciación

Actividad F Pronunciación: *La h, la y, la ll*

The **h** in Spanish is silent. It is never pronounced. Listen and repeat after the speaker.

h
hijo   hermano   hotel   hace   higiénico   hostal

Y in Spanish can be either a vowel or a consonant. As a vowel, it is pronounced exactly the same as the vowel **i**. Listen and repeat after the speaker.

y
Juan y María   el jabón y el champú

Y is a consonant when it begins a word or a syllable. As a consonant, **y** is pronounced similarly to the *y* in the English word *yo-yo*. This sound has several variations throughout the Spanish-speaking world. Listen and repeat after the speaker.

ya   desayuno   ayuda   playa

The **ll** is considered a single consonant in Spanish. In many areas of the Spanish-speaking world, it is pronounced the same as the **y**. It too has several variations. Listen and repeat after the speaker.

llama   cepillo   botella   toalla
llega   rollo   pastilla   lluvia

La hermana habla hoy con su hermano en el hotel.
Está lloviendo cuando ella llega al hostal en la calle Hidalgo.
El hombre lleva una botella de agua a la playa hermosa.

Lectura

Actividad G Listen.

SEGUNDA PARTE

Actividad A Listen and choose.

_____

_____

_____

_____

_____

_____

_____

Capítulo 13
Un viaje en tren

PRIMERA PARTE

Vocabulario — PALABRAS 1

Actividad A Listen and repeat.

Actividad B Listen and choose.

_____   _____   _____

_____   _____

Actividad C Listen and choose.

1. a b c   4. a b c

2. a b c   5. a b c

3. a b c   6. a b c

Actividad D Listen and choose.

1. sí   no   3. sí   no   5. sí   no

2. sí   no   4. sí   no   6. sí   no

Vocabulario   PALABRAS 2

Actividad E Listen and repeat.

Actividad F Listen and choose.

1. sí   no   4. sí   no   7. sí   no

2. sí   no   5. sí   no   8. sí   no

3. sí   no   6. sí   no   9. sí   no

Actividad G Listen and choose.

1. a   b   3. a   b   5. a   b   7. a   b

2. a   b   4. a   b   6. a   b   8. a   b

Estructura

Actividad A Listen and choose.

1. a   b   c   3. a   b   c   5. a   b   c

2. a   b   c   4. a   b   c   6. a   b   c

Actividad B Listen and answer.

1. a las siete   3. en tren   5. Emilio

2. a las cinco   4. en el Talgo   6. en segunda

Actividad C Listen and choose.

1. a   b   c   3. a   b   c   5. a   b   c

2. a   b   c   4. a   b   c   6. a   b   c

Actividad D Listen and choose.

1. presente   pasado   6. presente   pasado
2. presente   pasado   7. presente   pasado
3. presente   pasado   8. presente   pasado
4. presente   pasado   9. presente   pasado
5. presente   pasado   10. presente   pasado

Actividad E Listen and speak.

1. que no   3. que no   5. que van a perder
2. que no saben   4. que van a ganar

Conversación

Actividad F Listen

Actividad G Listen and choose.

1. sí no   4. sí no   7. sí no   10. sí no
2. sí no   5. sí no   8. sí no
3. sí no   6. sí no   9. sí no

Pronunciación

Actividad H Pronunciación: *La consonante ñ y la combinación ch*

The **ñ** is a separate letter of the Spanish alphabet. The mark over it is called a **tilde**. Note that it is pronounced similarly to the *ny* in the English word *canyon*. Listen and repeat after the speaker.

señor   otoño   España
señora   pequeño   cumpleaños
año

Ch is pronounced much like the *ch* in the English word *church*. Listen and repeat after the speaker.

coche   chocolate   chaqueta   muchacho

El señor español compra un coche cada año en el otoño.
El muchacho chileno duerme en una cama pequeña en el coche-cama.
La muchacha pequeña lleva una chaqueta color chocolate.

Lectura

Actividad I Listen.

SEGUNDA PARTE

Actividad A Listen.

Actividad B Listen and write.

1. Where is this conversation probably taking place?

   _____

2. What kind of ticket does Gerardo have?

   _____

3. When does Gerardo plan to return?

   _____

4. How much is a one-way ticket?

   _____

5. How much is a round-trip ticket?

   _____

6. What does the young woman suggest?

   _____

Actividad C Listen and write.

	Hora	Destino	Andén
1.	_____	_____	_____
2.	_____	_____	_____
3.	_____	_____	_____
4.	_____	_____	_____
5.	_____	_____	_____

Capítulo 14
En el restaurante

<svg>❖❖❖❖❖❖❖❖❖❖❖❖❖❖❖❖❖❖❖❖❖❖❖❖❖❖❖❖❖❖</svg>

PRIMERA PARTE

Vocabulario   PALABRAS 1

Actividad A Listen and repeat.

Actividad B Listen and choose.

1. sí no	**4.** sí no	**7.** sí no	**10.** sí no
2. sí no	**5.** sí no	**8.** sí no	
3. sí no	**6.** sí no	**9.** sí no	

Actividad C Listen and choose.

1. sí no	**4.** sí no	**7.** sí no
2. sí no	**5.** sí no	**8.** sí no
3. sí no	**6.** sí no	**9.** sí no

Actividad D Listen and choose.

1. a b c   5. a b c

2. a b c   6. a b c

3. a b c   7. a b c

4. a b c

Vocabulario   PALABRAS 2

Actividad E Listen and repeat.

Actividad F Listen and choose.

	Carne	Pescado	Marisco	Vegetal
1.	_____	_____	_____	_____
2.	_____	_____	_____	_____
3.	_____	_____	_____	_____
4.	_____	_____	_____	_____
5.	_____	_____	_____	_____
6.	_____	_____	_____	_____
7.	_____	_____	_____	_____
8.	_____	_____	_____	_____
9.	_____	_____	_____	_____
10.	_____	_____	_____	_____

Actividad G Listen and choose.

_____

_____

_____

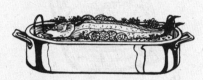

_____

_____

_____

Actividad H Listen and choose.

1. sí no   **3.** sí no   **5.** sí no

2. sí no   **4.** sí no   **6.** sí no

Estructura

Actividad A Listen and choose.

1. a b c   **6.** a b c

2. a b c   **7.** a b c

3. a b c   **8.** a b c

4. a b c   **9.** a b c

5. a b c

Actividad B Listen and answer.

1.

2.

3.

4.

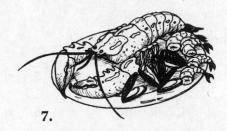

5.

6.

7.

Conversación

Actividad C Listen.

Actividad D Listen and choose.

1. a b c

2. a b c

3. a b c

4. a b c

5. a b c

Pronunciación

Actividad E Pronunciación: *La consonante x*

An **x** between two vowels is ponounced much like the English *x* but a bit softer. It's like a **gs: examen** > **eg-samen.** Listen and repeat after the speaker.

exacto	examen
éxito	próximo

When **x** is followed by a consonant, it is often pronounced like an **s.** Listen and repeat after the speaker.

extremo	explicar
exclamar	

El extranjero exclama que baja en la próxima parada.

Lectura

Actividad F Listen.

SEGUNDA PARTE

Actividad A Read.

Restaurante y Bar
La India Bonita
DESDE 1933

Cuernavaca, Mor.

" Cliente Distinguido "
Recibirá 10% de descuento
solo pago en efectivo en comidas y cenas
con bebidas.

Nº 2943

Dwight Morrow 106-B (Casa Mañana) 62000 Cuernavaca, Mor.
Tels. Fax 18-69-67 12-50-21

Actividad B Listen and choose.

1. sí   no   3. sí   no   5. sí   no

2. sí   no   4. sí   no

Actividad C Listen.

Actividad D Listen and choose.

1. ¿De qué trata el anuncio?

   a. Del sol.

   b. De un viaje.

   c. De un restaurante.

2. ¿Dónde está el Sol?

   a. En Cuba.

   b. En el centro de la ciudad.

   c. En todos los países hispanos.

3. ¿Qué tipo de comida sirven?

   a. Solamente comida hispana.

   b. Solamente comida cubana.

   c. Solamente comida mexicana.

4. ¿Cuál es la especialidad los martes?

   a. Masitas de cerdo a la cubana.

   b. Paella valenciana.

   c. Enchiladas de México.

5. ¿Qué se puede hacer por teléfono?

   a. Reservaciones.

   b. Paella.

   c. Pagar.